ANNUAL  2020

UK POLITICS

Nick Gallop

HODDER
EDUCATION
AN HACHETTE UK COMPANY

Acknowledgements

Every effort has been made to trace all copyright holders, but if any have been inadvertently overlooked, the Publishers will be pleased to make the necessary arrangements at the first opportunity.

Although every effort has been made to ensure that website addresses are correct at time of going to press, Hodder Education cannot be held responsible for the content of any website mentioned in this book. It is sometimes possible to find a relocated web page by typing in the address of the home page for a website in the URL window of your browser.

Hachette UK's policy is to use papers that are natural, renewable and recyclable products and made from wood grown in well-managed forests and other controlled sources. The logging and manufacturing processes are expected to conform to the environmental regulations of the country of origin.

Orders: please contact Bookpoint Ltd, 130 Park Drive, Milton Park, Abingdon, Oxon OX14 4SE. Telephone: +44 (0)1235 827827. Fax: +44 (0)1235 400401. E-mail education@bookpoint.co.uk Lines are open from 9 a.m. to 5 p.m., Monday to Saturday, with a 24-hour message answering service. You can also order through our website: www.hoddereducation.co.uk

ISBN: 978 1 5104 7219 8

First published in 2020 by

Hodder Education,

An Hachette UK Company

Carmelite House

50 Victoria Embankment

London EC4Y 0DZ

www.hoddereducation.co.uk

Impression number   10 9 8 7 6 5 4 3 2 1

Year   2024 2023 2022 2021 2020

Cover photo © Adobe Stock

Typeset in India

Printed by CPI Group (UK) Ltd, Croydon, CR0 4YY

A catalogue record for this title is available from the British Library.

MIX
Paper from responsible sources
FSC™ C104740

Contents

Contents

Chapter 1

Has Brexit won the case for codifying the UK's constitution?

Exam success

The UK constitution is a major topic within the examination specification and covers a wide range of historical milestones, political and institutional developments, and recent reforms. Effective answers to short, extract- and essay-based questions will need to weave together constitutional principles, contemporary events and precise knowledge of a substantial number of key terms — parliamentary sovereignty, the rule of law, statute and common law, and the differences between entrenched and unentrenched, codified and uncodified constitutions. The best candidates will be able to analyse the strengths and weaknesses of the UK's current constitutional arrangements in light of ongoing developments and, with reference to constitutional changes since 1997 and the challenges of Brexit, evaluate the arguments for and against further reform including the possibility of the UK's constitution becoming both entrenched and codified.

The up-to-date facts, examples and arguments in this chapter will help you to produce good quality answers in your AS unit tests in the following areas of the specifications:

Edexcel	UK Government 1.1–1.4	The constitution
AQA	3.1.1.1	The nature and sources of the British constitution

Context

For many, the 'unwritten' constitution is a distinctive and distinguishing feature of Britain's heritage. Conventional wisdom has it that while other seemingly less self-assured nations had to codify their political rules and relationships, their constitutional checks and balances, the UK had no such need. Not only this, but for supporters of the constitution, the UK has positively thrived for centuries with its loose, flexible collection of conventions and arrangements; provisions that have allowed for evolutionary change, responsible government and the gradual acceptance of new structures and procedures, all beneath the guiding supremacy of a sovereign parliament.

Events in the aftermath of the 2016 Brexit referendum appear to tear up this long-standing narrative. Instead of having a clear framework to steer a country calmly through a complicated political process, the UK's undefined constitutional arrangements seem to have done the reverse: to have magnified division and discord; to have been the cause of political and constitutional confusion.

The referendum may have provided a mandate for Brexit, but the process and terms by which departure were to take place were neither agreed nor understood. The UK's constitutional arrangements provided little clarity on basic procedural matters, such as whether Parliament or the government should take the lead. For many, Brexit has exposed the weaknesses — ambiguity, flexibility — of what were once considered to be the UK's constitutional strengths. For others, Brexit represents a unique and existential crisis that no amount of constitutional tidiness could have resolved easily.

In 2019, constitutional matters were widely considered to have reached crisis point. During the year, the UK government endured repeated defeats and protracted struggles for control of the parliamentary agenda. There were accusations of partisanship levelled at the House of Commons speaker, opposition-backed bills to force the government's negotiating stance, and a Supreme Court ruling on Parliament's prorogation that appeared to challenge the most fundamental constitutional doctrine of parliamentary sovereignty. All of this and more put the UK's constitutional arrangements under more pressure than at any previous time. Previous debates about codification may have been largely hypothetical, but 2019 saw arguments to codify the UK's constitutional arrangements become increasingly compelling.

Box 1.1 Key definitions

Parliamentary sovereignty: a central constitutional principle holding that Parliament is the supreme political and legislative body in the UK. While it might be convenient for other institutions to wield power (e.g. the devolved bodies) they do so under the authority of Parliament. In practical terms, the dominance of the executive, the process of devolution and membership of the EU have all substantially eroded parliamentary sovereignty.

Constitutions: seek to establish and define the framework of a state, how it is organised and the regulations, rights and principles that underpin it. A **codified constitution**, such as that of the USA, is set out in a single authoritative document. The US constitution was drawn up at the 1787 Philadelphia Convention and came into force 2 years later. It has been amended just 27 times in well over two centuries. An **uncodified constitution** is not necessarily unwritten; it is just not set out in a single document.

The UK's constitutional arrangements: these are uncodified, although most of them are written down in the form of Statute Law (Acts of Parliament that legally set out the framework and responsibilities of the state). However, constitutional arrangements are also to be found in the UK's vast body of common law (precedent-setting decisions made by judges in court), in various historical documents such as the Magna Carta and in works of authority such as Erskine May's *Parliamentary Practice*. Certain aspects of the UK's constitution are indeed 'unwritten'. These come in the form of widely accepted conventions such as collective cabinet responsibility.

The road to Brexit: from political drama to constitutional crisis

Post-2016, the years of Brexit negotiations could be likened to trench warfare: prolonged periods of inactivity punctuated occasionally by flashes of chaotic, often futile, action. To understand why the UK spent several years lurching between these two extremes, it is necessary to understand something of the background to the crisis.

Britain's entry to the Union was a controversial one. After two earlier attempts to join had been vetoed by French opposition, when membership was finally achieved on 1 January 1973 it was to an organisation that had been functioning for the benefit of its existing members for almost two decades.

Membership had not featured in the Conservative Party's election manifesto of 1970, and the lack of an electoral mandate became a significant political issue when the Labour Party promised a referendum if it won the next general election. In the event, and pertinent to contemporary events, the promise of a referendum became an important vote winner, and the ensuing referendum process proved to be a convenient way of resolving internal party debate.

Box 1.2 Why do people still disagree over EU membership?

Advocates of the EU sit right across the traditional left–right political spectrum. They stress the many social, economic and political advantages of continued membership. The HM Treasury estimates that up to 3 million jobs are linked to the UK's membership of the EU; and the freedom to travel, study and work in other EU countries is enjoyed by millions more. For supporters of the EU, the UK's economy, its security, global standing and the rights of its citizens, are all enhanced and protected by continued EU membership.

However, opposition to the developing European 'project' has simmered for more than 50 years, stemming from deeply rooted ideological conflicts within both main parties:

- For many on the left, there has been a long-standing aversion to the free market forces of the EU, believing it to jeopardise the stability of established workforces. Genuine political solidarity between nations, as advocated by Marx, has been replaced by supranational institutions (ones that reach across national borders in the interests of free trade) which serve business elites at the expense of the working classes (see Box 1.3).
- For many on the right, 'Euroscepticism' has become a passionate political stance (see Box 1.4). Eurosceptics believe that the EU fundamentally undermines national sovereignty, encourages high levels of migration which causes social breakdown, and supports institutions that are overly bureaucratic, expensive, inefficient and that lack democratic legitimacy.

Tony Benn was a staunch campaigner against the EU (then the EEC), stating during the 1975 referendum that remaining in the organisation would see 'half a million jobs lost in Britain and a huge increase in food prices'. The 1979 and 1983 Labour manifestos favoured British withdrawal from the EEC.

More recently, commentators on the left have highlighted the free-market downsides of the EU. Owen Jones wrote a 2015 *Guardian* article on why 'the left must put Britain's EU withdrawal on the agenda'. In the same year George Monbiot claimed that 'everything good about the EU is in retreat; everything bad is on the rampage'.

Box 1.4 **Euroscepticism and the 'right'**

Anti-EU sentiments on the right of the spectrum crystallised in 1988 when the Prime Minister and Conservative Party leader Margaret Thatcher warned of 'a European super-state exercising a new dominance in Brussels'.

In the 1990s, former Tory-backer Sir James Goldsmith formed the Referendum Party as a single-issue party to fight the 1997 general election, calling for a referendum on the UK's relationship with the EU. It briefly held a parliamentary seat when George Gardiner, the Conservative MP for Reigate, changed parties in March 1997 following a battle against deselection by his local party. In 1997, the Referendum Party received over 800,000 votes and finished fourth, but failed to win a seat in the House of Commons.

More recently, Douglas Carswell became the UK's first UKIP MP when he defected from the Conservatives in 2014. The 'Grassroots Out' campaign, launched in January 2016, was a cross-party alliance driven by founding Conservative MPs Peter Bone and Tom Pursglove.

In the following decades, resistance to EU membership from across the political and social spectrum was fuelled by the perception that the economic conveniences of the single market were steadily outweighed by the EU's ever-extending reach into national matters.

The victory of the Leave campaign in 2016 is often explained as the result of a complicated blend of sentiments ranging from misgivings about the legitimacy of EU institutions — and the extent to which they truly worked for the benefit of the UK and its citizens — to a pervading sense of personal and collective disempowerment. On a political level, loss of national control was salient among Leave voters, and on a social level the perceived transformation of communities by unexpected levels of immigration in the wake of the EU's eastward enlargement from 2004 was prominent.

The referendum campaign was also characterised by a failure on the part of the then government to communicate the full benefits of EU membership. It would be fair to say that the Leave victory came as a shock to almost all, not least those in government. 2019 saw the consequences of an unexpected and unplanned for result reach the proportions of a political and constitutional crisis.

Why has Brexit put so much strain on the UK's constitution?

The UK's vote to leave the EU has dominated the political landscape since 2016: several years of political and constitutional paralysis, parliamentary hostility, inter-party clashes and regional disputes. In fact, the process to agree whether, and how, the UK was to leave the EU has left virtually no constitutional principle, political process or institution of state – including the monarchy – untouched.

Ten ways in which Brexit has caused constitutional conflict include:

1 The constitutional position of referendums is unclear as they are a feature of direct democracy at odds with the UK's system of representative democracy. The transfer of direct involvement in the decision-making process may well be imperfect but results in the creation of a representative assembly that is regularly held to account by the electorate. The lack of any mechanism to hold to account a referendum decision – seemingly at any time in the future – has become all too apparent.

2 The European Union Referendum Act 2015 sanctioned the holding of the 2016 vote, but the vast majority of the Act dealt with the mechanics of how the vote would be conducted (such as voter eligibility and the role of the Electoral Commission). Unlike Ireland's constitution, in which Article 46 requires detailed proposals to be passed by the legislative body then voted upon, detailed legislative and constitutional plans were never drawn up to explain how the UK would implement the result of a Leave vote.

3 The legitimacy of the outcome itself is questionable. The infrequency of national referendums in the UK means that some voters view them as rare opportunities to deliver messages of wider dissatisfaction to the political establishment. Additionally, there remains intense concern over misleading campaign messaging and disagreement about whether the referendum result was advisory or legally binding (see Box 1.6).

4 The flexible relationships within the UK's multinational union have come under increasing strain as the devolved regions assert their rights to define a future relationship with the EU and to lay claim to repatriated powers. To add to the sense of imbalance and constitutional tension, Scotland voted Remain by 62–38%, in contrast to the 52–48% Leave vote in the UK as a whole.

5 Northern Ireland is at the forefront of the Brexit deadlock – a wholly unforeseen development for most politicians and voters alike. The fragility of powersharing (the agreement that powers are exercised by the Stormont government if the requirements to include a coalition across sectarian divides are met) and peace in the region has been magnified by the possibility of a post-Brexit 'hard border' with the Republic. In contravention of the Good Friday Agreement and other constitutional commitments, for a deal to be reached, Northern Ireland remaining in the customs union is regularly cited as the price to be paid, but one that the Democratic Unionists Party (DUP), with its strong Westminster presence, is deeply opposed to.

6 The UK courts have been drawn into the political fray too, being required to scrutinise and rule on a number of aspects of the Brexit process, thereby politicising the judicial function. In *R (Miller)* v *Secretary of State for Exiting the European Union* (2017) the UK Supreme Court ruled that the government could not appeal against a lower court ruling that the approval of Parliament was required prior to initiating the UK's withdrawal from the EU. In *R (Miller)* v *The Prime Minister* and *Cherry* v *Advocate General for Scotland* (2019), Brexit disagreement was widely seen as being behind Boris Johnson's decision to prorogue Parliament for up to 5 weeks – a prorogation that was ruled 'unlawful' by the Supreme Court in September 2019.

7 The prospect of the monarch being drawn into the Brexit conflict became very real in 2019. In August 2019 *The Spectator* asserted that 'one part of our unwritten constitution has been functioning perfectly during the Brexit process: the monarchy'. However, by granting the prime minister permission to prorogue Parliament in September – a move widely seen as an attempt to block further parliamentary discussion – sections of the public reacted by questioning the queen's little-known role in major public affairs.

8 Over the course of 2019, the effectiveness of the constitutional principle of parliamentary government was tested to the limit. For Parliament to function, an organised dominant party in possession of a healthy Commons majority is required. Without this, effective parliamentary government all but disappeared with the government defeated over the Withdrawal Agreement three times between January and March 2019.

9 Another key feature of the UK's constitutional arrangements is the accepted dominance of the executive over the legislative branch. Nineteenth-century constitutional expert Walter Bagehot's referred to this arrangement as the 'efficient secret' of the UK's constitution. On 4 September 2019, Boris Johnson's government had been defeated three times within 24 hours by the House of Commons as a no-deal Brexit was blocked and an attempt to force a snap general election failed. The inability of the executive to control the Commons, let alone dissolve it to trigger a general election, led to prolonged parliamentary paralysis and confusion.

10 The speaker of the House of Commons John Bercow admitted to voting Remain and has since been accused of using his prominent position to thwart the Brexit process. The lack of a governing majority, a basic required to control the House, drew the speaker into areas of parliamentary activity as never before (see Chapter 2). Whereas previously and by convention the speaker took on the role of neutral referee, in 2019 Bercow became highly influential and radical in shaping proceedings and outcomes.

While many supporters of the current uncodified arrangements assert that codification is not the answer, Britain is among a handful of states without an entrenched constitution.

Has Brexit won the case for codification?

The process of constitutional codification is widely considered likely to be an extraordinarily complicated and protracted task. Making it more difficult still, there is little appetite or enthusiasm for major constitutional upheaval and renewal, particularly amid ongoing Brexit uncertainties. Nevertheless, the arguments for reforming or retaining the UK's constitutional arrangements are seen to be more evenly balanced than at any previous time.

Table 1.1 Has Brexit won the case for codification?

YES	NO
Changing a fundamental constitutional provision following an advisory referendum that saw support from 36% of the total electorate (on a 72% turnout) is alarmingly easy. For many, Brexit has exposed the lack of protection inherent in the UK's constitutional arrangements.	A codified constitution would not necessarily have provided answers to the most pressing of questions about the legitimacy and status of the referendum result. Effective legislation — rather than constitutional codification — on the implications of the vote and the nature of the UK's departure from the EU would have provided this much needed clarity.

YES	NO
The Brexit process required the government to rely on out-dated and little understood political tools and processes — such as the royal prerogative and the intervention of the monarch — and forced the Supreme Court into the political arena to clarify matters. A codified constitution need not herald greater judicial activism, just sensible parliamentary provisions like super majorities.	A codified constitution would profoundly upset the relationship between the branches of government, handing even more power to the judicial branch. The Supreme Court's involvement in the Brexit process was helpful but limited — and appropriate to the precise circumstances at hand. A codified constitution freezes relationships and roles at any given time in a way that can rapidly become outmoded and unworkable.
The absence of legal safeguards for the powers of the devolved regions has become all too evident in the Brexit process. There is uncertainty about repatriated powers post-Brexit, and Scotland's and Northern Ireland's Remain vote has been ignored by the Westminster government, yet Brexit has serious implications for their future.	A codified constitution — not dissimilar to that of the USA — would still see the responsibility for international relations (such as a future relationship with the EU) lie in the hands of the central government in Westminster, and not with devolved regions or states, just as they would be in any federal arrangement.
The protection of rights is weak under the current arrangements. Rights legislation may well exist, but it is subject to the will and whim of Parliament and can be repealed at any moment. For example, the 2019 Withdrawal Act excludes the EU Charter of Fundamental Rights from UK law.	A good constitution provides effective checks and balances. If the Brexit process has proved anything it is that all three branches of government were required to play a part in 'delivering' it — not just one over-mighty branch. The Supreme Court required that Parliament trigger Article 50, and the executive has shaped the political and legislative parameters of the process.

Parallels, connections and comparisons

- Edmund Burke was a staunch defender of the British constitution's ability to adapt to even the most shocking of political 'moments'. Burke cited the seventeenth-century period from Civil War to regicide to Glorious Revolution, when 'England found itself without a king [but] did not, however, dissolve the whole fabric' of government. For Edmund Burke, insufficiently considered constitutional changes that have unexpectedly far-reaching effects — examples might include the Fixed-Term Parliaments Act that prevented a paralysed government from calling a general election — are to be avoided.
- The constitutions of the USA and UK are different in so many ways — not just in terms of their origins and nature but also structurally, as the US constitution is codified and entrenched. However, codification is not necessarily 'best', and even the US constitution has significant omissions, with no mention made of aspects of US politics that have taken on momentous importance such as those of judicial review, the work of congressional committees and the democratic significance of primary elections.

Summary

As demonstrated in this chapter, the UK's constitution is highly relevant to all other topics in the specification. Understanding the implications of parliamentary sovereignty on the relationships with the devolved bodies, the ever-changing constitutional relationship between the executive, legislative and judicial branches and the strength of the protection of individual rights and liberties is vital.

As well as analysis of the extent to which recent events have altered understandings of whether the UK should codify its constitution, the topic requires a thorough knowledge of:

- the sources and principles of the UK's constitution
- recent constitutional reforms and their effectiveness
- the protection of rights in the UK and the case for a British Bill of Rights

What next?

Read: the following highly informative academic blogs on the implications of Brexit for the UK constitution:

- 'Brexit: the constitution and the future of the UK' by Professor Vernon Bogdanor on the LSE's blog (**https://blogs.lse.ac.uk**)
- 'Will Brexit change the UK constitution?' on the Hansard Society's website (**www.hansardsociety.org.uk**)

Chapter 2

Did backbenchers 'take back control' of Parliament in 2019?

Exam success

Students are required to have a high level of knowledge and understanding of the roles and composition of both houses of Parliament and the ways that their functions differ. The examination specifications also place a strong emphasis on the relationship between the legislative and executive branches. The best answers will be able to deploy contemporary examples to explain the extent to which the balance of power between the legislature and executive evolved in 2019, and how the levels of accountability and scrutiny — of the government and of government ministers — changed. With this in mind, the power and influence of backbenchers in the House of Commons, and the support that they enjoyed from the speaker of the House of Commons, was one of the most prominent parliamentary developments of 2019.

| Edexcel | UK Government 2.4 | The ways in which Parliament interacts with the executive:
■ The role and significance of backbenchers in both Houses |
| AQA | 3.1.1.2 | The structure and role of Parliament:
■ Scrutiny of the executive and how effective scrutiny of the executive is in practice
■ The roles and influence of MPs |

Context

Backbenchers are MPs who sit in the House of Commons without ministerial (or frontbench) responsibility. As MPs they are most active in parliamentary committees, and much of their influence occurs prior to bills reaching Parliament, in the early formulation of legislation in areas in which they have interest and expertise.

Periods of relatively high party discipline and strong governing majorities see the danger of parliamentary revolt largely negated. For example, while Tony Blair did not experience a single parliamentary defeat in his first two terms in office (1997–2005), Theresa May's minority administration from 2017 to 2019 was defeated 33 times. In 2019, backbench rebellions moved from a distant threat to an everyday reality. Boris Johnson's working majority disappeared on the first parliamentary day of his tenure: his government was subsequently defeated six times in as many days between 3 and 9 September 2019. Not only that but the Opposition-backed European (Withdrawal) (No.2) Act 2019 (known variously as the 'Benn Act' or 'Surrender Act') was passed with unprecedented speed for a bill of its kind, being introduced on 3 September 2019 and given royal assent on 9 September 2019.

Facilitating the rise of backbenchers in 2019 was the speaker of the House of Commons.

John Bercow became the 157th speaker on 22 June 2009, succeeding Michael Martin in the aftermath of the parliamentary expenses scandal. As speaker of the House, Bercow immediately vowed to put the interests of backbenchers to the fore and his years in office saw a concerted campaign to redress the balance of power away from the executive and towards the legislature. He courted controversy on a number of occasions, not least when accused of breaking rules on impartiality after declaring Donald Trump unfit to address MPs in Westminster because Parliament was opposed to 'racism and sexism'.

Bercow, who stepped down after a decade in the speaker's chair on 31 October 2019, has been referred to as both 'backbench champion' and 'constitutional vandal'. Nevertheless, his efforts to check the power of the government made a substantial impact on parliamentary proceedings in 2019.

Box 2.1 Key definitions

Backbencher: an MP who does not hold front bench responsibilities, and is therefore not a minister or shadow minister. The term originates from the seating location in the House of Commons chamber of representatives who do not have specific responsibilities. While the threat of a backbench rebellion is only a reality in times of slender government majorities, evidence indicates that those MPs who differentiate themselves by rebelling frequently are more likely to make a lasting impression on voters.

Speaker of the House of Commons: the presiding officer in the chamber, maintaining order during debates, determining which members may speak, and ensuring that the rules of the House are maintained. The office of speaker is steeped in history and it is regarded as vital that the post-holder is non-partisan and able to command the respect of the whole chamber. John Bercow (speaker from 2009–19) billed himself as the 'backbencher's friend'. His successor, former deputy speaker and Labour MP Lindsay Hoyle, took office emphasising his objectives to be a 'transparent' speaker, and pledging to take the welfare of House of Commons staff seriously.

What role did backbenchers play in holding the government to account in 2019?

Backbenchers under May

In times of inflated government majorities, backbenchers are often referred to as 'lobby fodder', either voting with the government in overwhelming numbers or rebelling in small and largely meaningless protests. Early 2019 provided an entirely different environment for parliamentary relations, with several examples of backbenchers defeating or holding the government to account in unprecedented ways:

- On 15 January 2019, Theresa May's government was defeated by a 230-vote margin, the largest defeat of any prime minister in parliamentary history. After immediately tabling a no confidence vote, Labour leader Jeremy Corbyn told MPs: 'This is a catastrophic defeat. The house has delivered its verdict on her deal. Delay and denial have reached the end of the line.' Theresa May went on to survive the confidence vote the following day, by 325 votes to 306.
- On 25 March 2019, MPs voted by 327 votes to 300 to pass a motion which dictated that the following day would be set aside for MPs to put forward potential solutions as to the terms upon which the UK would leave the EU. In doing so, Parliament voted to take control of the parliamentary agenda in order to table and vote upon a range of possible solutions. However, no solution received a majority of support.
- On 29 March 2019, the government was defeated for a third time over Theresa May's Withdrawal Agreement. 34 Conservative backbench MPs voted against the bill, which ensured that the government lost by 58 votes.

Ultimately, Theresa May's working majority, which required the support of the Democratic Unionist Party, was undone by a small but determined number of backbench rebels who refused to support her stance on Brexit. Within 2 months of her March defeat May announced her resignation as Conservative Party leader and prime minister.

Backbenchers under Johnson

September 2019 saw events in Parliament move from merely 'unprecedented' to those which astonished even the most seasoned of assembly observers. A timeline of events reflects the flow of power away from government and towards Parliament. Ultimately, a rebellion of a small number of Conservative backbench MPs proved pivotal in events:

- On 28 August 2019, Boris Johnson announced that Parliament would be prorogued (suspended) for up to 5 weeks in order for the ministers to work on the government's legislative agenda which would be announced in the upcoming Queen's Speech on 14 October 2019.
- Between 28 August and 3 September, the prime minister's lengthy prorogation was widely condemned as being excessive and designed to suppress parliamentary debate of the Brexit process as the government headed for a likely 'no deal' on 31 October.
- On 3 September the speaker firstly permitted an emergency debate on the matter of prorogation and secondly allowed the fast-tracking of the European Union (Withdrawal) (No. 6) Bill which was supported by Conservative rebels and forced the government to request an extension to Brexit negotiations.
- In an attempt to undermine the parliamentary resistance, two government motions under the Fixed-term Parliaments Act 2011 calling for an early election both failed, well short of the required two-thirds majority required.

Boris Johnson's government was defeated by a small but significant number of Conservative backbenchers who voted against their party and with the Opposition in support of a move to prevent a no-deal Brexit. The government response was to expel the 21 rebel MPs from the parliamentary Conservative Party. The 21 expelled MPs included two ex-chancellors and a number of senior figures in both Theresa May's and David Cameron's governments, a small but highly influential band of backbenchers whose actions in 2019 changed the course of parliamentary history.

How did the speaker empower backbenchers?

As noted, the speaker took on a pivotal role in the parliamentary process of EU withdrawal. John Bercow's actions in the speaker's chair over the course of a decade, one which encompassed possibly the most tumultuous eras for Parliament in modern times, infuriated many on the government benches, within the Conservative Party, and in certain sections of the media. Bercow's detractors accused him of partisanship and constitutional trickery to thwart the will of the government, while his supporters, such as Labour leader Jeremy Corbyn, have praised him as a 'superb speaker' who had left Parliament 'stronger'.

Three particular incidents in 2019 illustrated the lengths that Speaker Bercow was prepared to go to curb or control the government:

- In March 2019, the speaker invoked a convention dating back to 1604 which stated that a vote on a motion that is 'substantially the same' as a rejected motion, should be blocked. Consequently, Theresa May's bid for a third vote on her withdrawal bill was not permitted until a significant part of the Bill — the Political Declaration (a 26-page document which set out the framework for the future relationship between the EU and the UK) — was removed. Nevertheless, the government lost the vote by 344 votes to 286.
- In early September 2019, the speaker vowed to 'rip up the parliamentary rule book', and to permit 'procedural creativity' in order to allow Parliament to block Boris Johnson from ignoring the law in his handling of the government's Brexit negotiations. In words that were widely considered to be uncharacteristically forthright for a speaker, Bercow stated: 'If I have been remotely ambiguous so far, let me make myself crystal clear. The only form of Brexit that we have, whenever that might be, will be a Brexit that the House of Commons has explicitly endorsed.'
- Following the UK Supreme Court ruling on 24 September 2019 that Boris Johnson's prorogation of Parliament was unlawful, the speaker immediately reacted by declaring that Parliament would reconvene the following day when there would be time for urgent questions and ministerial statements. In the days that followed, John Bercow largely controlled the business of the House from the speaker's chair in what opponents considered to be a breach of established parliamentary practice. Events intensified when in John Bercow's final days he refused a government request to hold a vote on its Brexit deal. The prime minister's official spokesman claimed that 'the speaker has yet again denied us a chance to deliver on the will of British people'.

> **Box 2.2** **Alternative media opinions of Speaker John Bercow**
>
> Far from being an even-handed defender of ordinary MPs, he was often biased, vindictive and hypocritical. No speaker in modern times has so shamelessly manipulated parliamentary convention to suit his own political preferences. His preparedness to jettison the traditional impartiality of the speaker and bend the rules to advance his own opinions was most visible over Brexit.
>
> Stephen Glover, *Daily Mail*, September 2019
>
> Bercow's instinct to empower parliament is real and consistent. Not only has he allowed MPs to seize control of proceedings from the government but colluded with them by widening the scope of emergency debates to allow parliamentary insurrections.
>
> James Butler, *Guardian*, September 2019

How has the use of 'urgent questions' checked the power of the government?

One of the most significant ways by which John Bercow sought to champion backbenchers and check the power of the government was through the use of urgent questions to ministers.

> **Box 2.3** **What are urgent questions to ministers?**
>
> An urgent question requires a government minister to come to the House of Commons Chamber and give an immediate answer without prior notice. An MP can apply to the speaker for an urgent question if he/she thinks a matter is urgent and important, and there is unlikely to be another way of raising it in the House. If the speaker agrees, the question is asked at the end of that day's question time.
>
> Source: **www.parliament.uk**

Under previous speakers the average number of urgent questions granted per parliamentary session barely made it into double figures (see Table 2.1). After 2010, and under Bercow, this figure leapt to an average of 49 per parliamentary session. From 2017 the number of urgent questions rose to 248 in a single — albeit very long — parliamentary session. The urgent questions raised in 2019 included those on the wider topics such as the Hong Kong protests, climate change and the future of British Steel, but the vast majority of them focused upon the government's handling of Brexit.

Table 2.1 Number of urgent questions granted by the speaker since 1997

Parliament	Number of parliamentary sessions	Total number of urgent questions per session	Average per number of urgent questions per parliamentary session
1997–2001	4	57	14
2001–05	4	40	10
2005–10	5	51	10
2010–15	4	196	49
2015–17	2	151	76
2017–19	1	248	248

Source: House of Commons Library, 2019

Examples of Brexit-related urgent questions to ministers in 2019 include:

- In March 2019, John Baron MP was granted an urgent question to Chris Heaton-Harris, parliamentary under-secretary of state for exiting the European Union, which required the minister to reveal greater details in order to provide reassurance that the government was preparing for the possibility of a no-deal Brexit. A six-page document – 'Operation Yellowhammer' – was published in September 2019.
- In June 2019, Alberto Costa MP was granted an urgent question on EU/British Citizens' rights. In an oral response in the Commons, EU minister Robin Walker reaffirmed 'that citizens' rights have been a priority throughout the negotiations and is an area that both the government and this House takes extremely seriously'.
- In September 2019, the shadow secretary of state for Northern Ireland, Tony Lloyd was granted an urgent question on the impact of Parliament's prorogation (suspension) on governance in Northern Ireland. The secretary of state for Northern Ireland, Julian Smith, was required to reassure the Commons that there would be 'a report on or before the 9 October to update on progress'.

There can be no doubting John Bercow's expansiveness in granting urgent questions. In the year before his accession just two were granted. In 2018, 152 were granted in a single year. The speaker's extensive granting of urgent questions has played a major part in what is widely seen as a reversal of power relations, with backbench MPs able to call ministers to account on an entirely unprecedented scale.

Parallels, connections and comparisons

- In the UK, the speaker resigns from his/her original party upon taking office and is usually unopposed by major parties in subsequent elections. However, in France and in Germany the speaker maintains an active involvement in party politics and in the US House of Representatives the equivalent role of speaker is highly partisan.

- In the USA, at the beginning of each new Congress, elections for House (of Representatives) speaker take place. On 3 January 2019, the House's 126th speaker election took place since the office was created in 1789. House Democratic leader Nancy Pelosi received a majority — with a vote split on part lines — to continue in the post. Like their UK-counterpart, the House speaker is the political and parliamentary leader of the House but, unlike the Commons speaker, the House speaker in the USA is second in the presidential line of succession after the vice president.
- Accusations of excessive partisanship are levelled at the US speaker just as they have been recently at the UK speaker. Nancy Pelosi has clashed on a number of occasions with President Trump, notably in 2019 over refusing to support funding for a border wall. Republican speaker John Boehner previously clashed with the Democrat president Barack Obama over healthcare reforms.

Summary

2019 saw a very different relationship develop between the legislature and the executive, largely down to the absence of a stable single party government, one that could withstand the pressure of the occasional small-scale backbench rebellion. Add to this the unique uncertainties of the Brexit process and an activist, expansionist Commons speaker and the scene was set for clashes, challenges and defeats on an extraordinary scale.

There are several other notable areas to consider when evaluating the relationship between the executive and the legislature including other forums for scrutiny that perhaps took something of a back seat in 2019 — the House of Lords and the work of select committees. In addition, the topic encourages students to fully consider:

- debates about the functions and the relative powers of the Commons and Lords in the various representative roles that both houses have
- the nature of the legislative process and the effectiveness of the government in controlling the stages of a bill
- the formal roles of the opposition in checking the power of the government

What next?

Read: Dr Emma Kilheeney's article 'Has Brexit empowered Parliament?' in *Politics Review*, Volume 29, Issue 3, which evaluates the relationship between Brexit and Parliament

Watch: 'The speaker [John Bercow] explains: granting urgent questions' on YouTube

Research: the Parliament briefing paper 'Number of urgent questions in the House of Commons since 1997' by Sarah Priddy, May 2019

Chapter 3

Prime minister and cabinet relations in 2019: from disunity to diversity?

Exam success

Students require a thorough knowledge and understanding of all aspects of the UK executive, a major topic within the examination specifications. The topic encompasses the roles and responsibilities, powers and constraints of the prime minister and his/her relationship with the cabinet, as well as the factors at play in the prime minister's selection of cabinet colleagues. The principles of collective and individual ministerial responsibility feature prominently. While it is important to be able to differentiate between these principles, the best candidates will be able to deploy examples in conjunction with the ebb and flow of prime ministerial power, relations between prime minister and cabinet, and the ability of the executive to influence events.

Edexcel	UK government 3.2 and 3.3	The concept of ministerial responsibility The prime minister and the cabinet: ■ The factors that affect the relationship between the cabinet and the prime minister
AQA	3.1.1.3	The prime minister and cabinet: ■ The relationship between the prime minister and cabinet ■ The difference between individual and collective cabinet responsibility

Context

2019 saw Theresa May's brief but turbulent premiership end. While her tenure will most specifically be remembered for her failure to 'deliver' an acceptable Brexit deal, a pledge she made when taking office in the summer of 2016, it will also be cited as a period of unprecedented executive turmoil, when some of the most significant practices of the British government (such as supporting and defending of government decisions in public) were either tested to the limit or jettisoned entirely.

Amid this, Theresa May developed a reputation for survival in the most difficult and intimidating of political circumstances. She was burdened by

the electoral misfire of 2017 — when she went to polls and lost 2015's hard-won government majority — and obstructed by the resignations of key staff and vital times — not only central figures such as Boris Johnson (foreign secretary) and David Davis (Brexit secretary) but also by the sheer number and frequency of them during what was one of the shortest prime ministerial tenures in the postwar period.

Collective responsibility may have been difficult to maintain during the period 2016–18, but as the vote on May's Withdrawal Bill neared, the principle appeared to have became untenable, and there were 19 ministerial resignations under Theresa May in the first 5 months of 2019 alone, with a further 6 immediately following the accession of Boris Johnson in June.

Box 3.1 Key definitions

The cabinet: the leading committee of government, comprising the senior secretaries of state and headed by the prime minister. The theory of 'cabinet government' emphasises the supremacy of the cabinet as a decision-making body, though the predominance of recent prime ministers, and their favouring of bilateral meetings and cabinet committees, has widely been seen as undermining the cabinet's decision-making status.

Collective ministerial responsibility: the principle that requires cabinet and government ministers to support government policy publicly, even if they disagree with the decision privately. If ministers cannot maintain collective responsibility, they must resign from their posts.

Individual ministerial responsibility: the principle that government ministers are singularly responsible for their conduct, their work government and their relationships with their colleagues. If a minister fails to meet the expectations demanded of high public office or is unable to reconcile personal issues or differences, resignation is required.

How destabilising were ministerial resignations under Theresa May in 2019?

The executive is one of three branches of government that sits alongside the legislature and the judiciary. Relations between and within these branches — in the UK and elsewhere — can fluctuate significantly as each plays a role in a system of 'checks and balances' that upholds respective constitutional principles and provides the basis for a healthy democracy.

A stable cabinet is the basis for the UK's parliamentary system. On a very basic level, the cabinet is an important policy-making and policy-deciding body. In times of crisis, that importance becomes vital, as the government needs to present a united and composed front. Additionally, for Parliament to function effectively, the cabinet must set an emphatic example of unity and stability — to the government and the parliamentary party too — in order to maintain control of the order and business of the House of Commons.

Box 3.2 How big is the cabinet?

In the UK, the size of the cabinet is deliberately imprecise, allowing the body to change and evolve depending on circumstances and priorities. For example in 2016, Theresa May appointed a specific cabinet position to lead the newly created Department for Exiting the European Union (DExEU). However, in order to maintain a workable 'committee', the number of cabinet ministers is usually restricted to around 23 (including the prime minister) and Boris Johnson's cabinet in September of 2019 comprised this number.

Relations within the executive (the cabinet and wider government) in Theresa May's final months in office were extremely fraught. In March 2019, 2 months before the prime minister announced her own plans to leave office, it was widely reported that there had been an irrecoverable government breakdown over Brexit. In the end, Theresa May was as much undone by her failure to garner wider support for an acceptable Brexit deal, as she was by her inability to maintain discipline and loyalty within her cabinet and government.

Three resignations in the space of 10 days in late March and early April 2019 illustrate the levels of disunity and conflict that the prime minister faced:

- Alister Burt, a minister in the Foreign Office, resigned on 25 March 2019 in opposition to the prospect of leaving the EU without a deal. Burt explained that 'having stretched the patience of collective responsibility recently' he felt unable to continue to support the government, and instead voted with the opposition in support of an amendment that would permit Parliament to take control of the Brexit process.
- Nigel Adams, parliamentary under-secretary of state for Wales, resigned on 3 April 2019 in protest at Theresa May making the 'calamity of a Corbyn government' more likely by opening talks with the Labour leader. Adams explained to the prime minister that 'legitimising and turning to Jeremy Corbyn to assist you at this crucial time, rather than being bold, is a grave error'.
- Chris Heaton-Harris, junior minister at the Department for Exiting the EU, became the 30th minister to resign from Theresa May's government on 4 April 2019, saying that his job had become 'irrelevant' because 'the prime minister does not intend to take the UK out of the EU without a deal' – a possibility that he had worked to prepare for. Heaton-Harris fervently opposed a further extension of Article 50.

So, ministerial resignations over Brexit occurred in quick succession because (a) leaving 'with a deal' did not look likely, (b) leaving with 'no deal' was not more confidently embraced by the government, and (c) efforts to avoid a 'no deal' by holding cross-party talks were opposed – an impossibly conflicted state of affairs for any prime minister to navigate successfully.

However, May's 3-year tenure encompassed more ministerial resignations than either Tony Blair or Margaret Thatcher experienced in their 10 years in office.

Indeed Gavin Freeguard in *Prospect Magazine* (May 2019) emphasises the unprecedented scale and scope of the resignations, pointing out that:

> Between 1979 and 2017, only once did three ministers resign in the same 24-hour period (Carrington, Atkins and Luce over the Falklands). This has happened three times since the start of 2018 — three ministers in July 2018, four in November 2018, and three this week [March 2019] — because of Brexit.

The destructiveness of repeated resignations thoroughly destabilised the prime minister. In many cases, the resignation of a cabinet minister was closely followed by those of junior ministers in their departments, leading to further confusion not just for the individual departments of state but as an increasing number of posts were unfilled, for the government and the country.

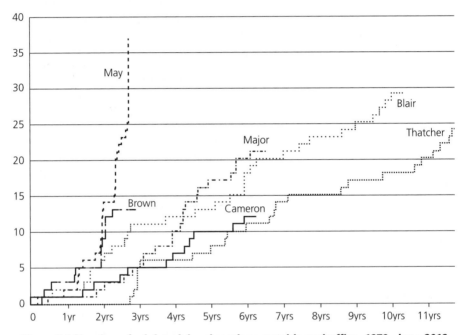

Figure 3.1 Number of ministerial resignations outside reshuffles, 1979–June 2019

Source: Institute for Government

Note: there were a further six resignations prior to Johnson taking office.

Case study 1: Andrea Leadsom resigns following a 'complete breakdown of collective ministerial responsibility', 22 May 2019

Just 2 days before Theresa May announced the schedule for her own resignation and replacement, Andrea Leadsom, the leader of the House of Commons, resigned. Her resignation letter (below) cited four reasons, explicitly referenced what she termed 'a complete breakdown of collective responsibility' in the government and explained that she was no longer able to support the government's approach to delivering Brexit. The resignation of a such a high profile minister was considered to be a near fatal blow to the prime minister who, at the time, was resisting intense pressure to step aside.

Excerpt from Andrea Leadsom's resignation letter to Theresa May (May 2019):

I no longer believe that our approach will deliver on the referendum result, for the following reasons:

1 I do not believe that we will be a truly sovereign United Kingdom through the deal that is now proposed;

2 I have always maintained that a second referendum would be dangerously divisive, and I do not support the government willingly facilitating such a concession. It would also risk undermining our union which is something I passionately want to see strengthened;

3 There has been such a breakdown of government processes that recent Brexit-related legislative proposals have not been properly scrutinised or approved by cabinet members;

4 The tolerance to those in cabinet who have advocated policies contrary to the government's position has led to a complete breakdown of collective responsibility.

What was the impact of early ministerial resignations under Boris Johnson?

Theresa May experienced one of the highest numbers of front bench resignations under any leadership. May's premiership lasted a little over 3 years, yet she faced 43 cabinet or government ministerial resignations during that time. These figures may be less than surprising given the context that many of the resignations were from ministers unable to support the government's stance on EU membership withdrawal – including two Brexit secretaries.

However, Boris Johnson was certainly not immune from ministerial resignations and the first rush of them came immediately on him taking office. In the 2 days between 22 and 24 July, there were eight resignations:

- Andrew Percy, prime ministerial trade envoy to Canada, resigned on 22 July over opposition to how no-deal Brexit policies would harm UK–Canada trade.
- Alan Duncan, minister of state for Europe and the Americas, resigned on 22 July in opposition to the incoming prime minister's acceptance of a no-deal Brexit.
- Anne Milton, minister of state for apprenticeships and skills, resigned on 23 July due to 'grave concerns' over Boris Johnson's Brexit policies.
- Philip Hammond, chancellor of the exchequer, resigned on 24 July, over Boris Johnson's willingness to leave the EU without a deal (see Case study 2).
- David Gauke, secretary of state for justice resigned on 24 July over Boris Johnson's willingness to leave the EU without a deal.
- Rory Stewart OBE, secretary of state for international development, resigned on 24 July over Boris Johnson's willingness to leave the EU without a deal.

- David Lidington, chancellor of the Duchy of Lancaster, resigned on 24 July over Boris Johnson's willingness to leave the EU without a deal, as well as believing it was 'time to leave the frontbench'.
- Lord Taylor of Holbeach, government chief whip in the House of Lords, resigned on 24 July over an issue independent of the 'political situation' having planned to resign for a long time beforehand.

Case study 2: Philip Hammond's resignation, 24 July 2019

In a rash of early resignations following the accession of Boris Johnson, Philip Hammond, the chancellor of the exchequer, was the most prominent minister to depart from the government on 24 July 2019, addressing his resignation letter to outgoing Prime Minister Theresa May on her final day in office. Hammond was among 17 senior ministers to resign, with fellow MP Nigel Evans describing it as a 'not so much a reshuffle as a summer's day massacre'. Hammond said that he was determined to block a no-deal Brexit from outside the government.

An excerpt from Philip Hammond's resignation letter to Theresa May:

> I believe that your successor must be free to choose a chancellor who is fully aligned with his policy position.

Despite the particularly feverish Westminster mood in the summer of 2019, it is not unusual for significant changes to take place when new prime ministers assume office. Then, the incoming prime minister May was acclaimed for unveiling a 'new look cabinet', after sacking George Osborne, Michael Gove, John Whittingdale, Nicky Morgan and Oliver Letwin.

In the months following Johnson's accession, and against a backdrop of significant media criticism, parliamentary hostility and an adverse ruling by the Supreme Court to thwart his prorogation plans, the newly formed cabinet remained relatively stable. The resignations of Jo Johnson (see Case study 3) and Amber Rudd (see Case study 4) were not the catalyst for further departures.

Case study 3: Jo Johnson's resignation, 5 September 2019

Examples of resignations on the grounds of individual ministerial responsibility in 2019 include that of Jo Johnson, the former transport secretary and brother of the prime minister. While there were significant elements of being unable to reconcile his own views on Brexit with the course that the government was taking, it was the 'unresolvable tension' within the family, meaning that personal strain and hostility towards his older brother's leadership was at the heart of the resignation and rendered him incapable of serving within the cabinet.

Excerpt from a tweet by Jo Johnson, resigning from the government:

> In recent weeks I've been torn between family loyalty and the national interest—it's an unresolvable tension and time for others to take on my roles as MP & minister. #overandout

extremely rare', and KV was **granted the right to appeal** which gave important guidance on the treatment of expert medical evidence in asylum cases.

- In July 2019 in the case of *Secretary of State for Work and Pensions* v *MM* (2019) the Supreme Court was required to determine whether a man in his forties who was denied an allowance paid to certain people with long-term health problems or disability was eligible to appeal this decision. The Court **clarified the meaning of the law**, specifically certain clauses within the Welfare Reform Act 2012.

Should judges have ruled on Parliament's prorogation?

On 1 October 2009 the Supreme Court took its place at the top of the UK's judicial system. There was moderation and reassurance from one of its new justices, Lady Hale, who explained at the time:

> Our jurisdiction will be the same. Our powers will be the same. We won't get any greater or grander powers by becoming the Supreme Court of the United Kingdom.

Almost exactly 10 years later, on 24 September 2019, it was Lady Hale again — now Chief Justice of the Supreme Court — who delivered a ruling in *R (Miller)* v *The Prime Minister* and *Cherry* v *Advocate General for Scotland* (2019) after the prime minister's decision to prorogue (suspend) Parliament was challenged. Lady Hale explained in paragraph 50 of the judgement:

> A decision to prorogue parliament (or to advise the monarch to prorogue Parliament) will be unlawful if the prorogation has the desired effect of frustrating or preventing, without reasonable justification, the ability of Parliament to carry out its constitutional functions as a legislature and as the body responsible for supervising the electorate.

Box 4.3   Questions the Court decided concerning Parliament's prorogation

The Court had two questions to decide:

- First, the judges had to determine whether the prorogation was justiciable: was it the role of the Court to rule on whether the prime minister's decision was lawful? The Supreme Court decided it was. It is a question of law, the Supreme Court said, where the limits of the power to prorogue lie. If the power had no legal limits at all, then the prime minister would be able to suspend Parliament for as long as he pleased — and that, said the Court, would be inconsistent with parliamentary sovereignty.
- Second, the Court had to decide whether this particular prorogation was lawful. The Court did not take a view on Boris Johnson's motive for prorogation; instead it focused on the prorogation's effect.

Source: 'The Supreme Court has fortified Parliament's "constitutional role" — and its own', Raphael Hogarth, 25 September 2019, www.instituteforgovernment.org.uk

---

For some, the Supreme Court's ruling — framed as a 'one off', and under circumstances that are 'unlikely to ever happen again' — was appropriate. It was the Court delivering an exceptional verdict at a time of national and political crisis on the lawfulness of the prime minister's decision to close parliament for what was, by all measures, a remarkably long period of time.

For others, regardless of the wisdom or even the legitimacy of a lengthy parliamentary prorogation, the willingness of the Court to appoint itself arbiter of the constitutional actions of the prime minister and the government represents a momentous development. From now on, critics argue, the exercise of the prerogative, hitherto restrained only by parliament itself, is subject to the approval of the UK Supreme Court.

Either way, the Court's ruling has implications not just for the UK, but for other Westminster-style and Commonwealth systems where the 'power to prorogue' is highly likely to be affected by this judgement. As far as the UK is concerned, the ruling reflects the developing role of the court and the establishment of its power to determine what is constitutionally proper behaviour and what is not.

According to The Institute for Government, two particular outcomes from the ruling were noted as follows:

1 Parliament's role in holding the government to account is part of the UK's constitutional law — and if the government threatens that accountability, then the courts will move to protect it.

2 The judges' language and reasoning — as well as their ultimate conclusion — shows that the Supreme Court now sees itself as a 'constitutional court' whose role is to protect democracy.

Box 4.4 The Case of Proclamations (1610)

Is there precedence for the Supreme Court checking the prerogative? Over 400 years ago Sir Edward Coke ruled that King James I was not able to stop new building in London, unless he was supported by Parliament. At the time, the king believed in his divine right to make any law he wished. The court opposed his view, deciding that the monarchy could not wield its power in this arbitrary way. By the end of the century, the Glorious Revolution had laid the foundation for today's constitutional monarchy.

Table 4.1 Should judges have ruled on Parliament's prorogation?

YES	NO
It is the responsibility of judges to apply the law and determine the constitutional principles that underpin it. As the Supreme Court explained, the effect of the prorogation was to prevent Parliament carrying out its constitutional function. The Court explained that this constituted an 'improper purpose' for prorogation.	The Divisional Court had previously ruled that the prime minster was acting within the law to prorogue parliament in the way that he had wanted. Yet this considered decision was swept aside by an 'activist' Supreme Court, citing precedents from 400 years ago but policing the powers of the prime minister in a completely new way for the modern era.
Traditionally, only a few days are needed to prepare for the Queen's Speech. The prime minister's prorogation for 5 weeks (albeit including the party conferences) was unsupported: '...no justification for taking such action with such an extreme effect has been put before the court'.	Points of law are often based upon what a 'reasonable person' might think. In a standard year, the House of Commons is largely inactive during the party conference period and for the several days prior to a Queen's Speech. So, Boris Johnson's proposed prorogation covered this period and a little more — at an exceptionally busy time for an incoming prime minister. Some would consider the length of the prorogation to be 'reasonable'.
The Court considered the advice Boris Johnson gave to the queen to be unlawful, concluding that 'it is impossible for us to conclude... that there was any reason — let alone a good reason' for the prime minister's request to prorogue. For many, the real reason was to thwart further parliamentary debate of the Brexit process — not to 'prepare for the Queen's Speech' at all.	Parliament's prorogation was cancelled on 24 September 2019 and within a day of the ruling was sitting again. However, no specific developments to the UK's negotiating position occurred in the days that followed, and yet the Supreme Court declared that had parliament remained prorogued, it would have had 'an extreme effect on the fundamentals of our democracy'.
The government is taken to court more often than many people realise. The Supreme Court deals on a regular basis with cases involving the actions of ministers and government departments. This ruling may have been very high profile, but the Court's behaviour is in keeping with precedent.	The Court has decided to encroach on matters that are the preserve of the executive. Parliament enjoys democratic legitimacy, unelected judges do not. The Supreme Court should have encouraged Parliament to bring forward legislation formalising the process (and duration) of prorogation. It should not have ruled upon it.

Parallels, connections and comparison

- The UK's uncodified constitutional arrangements mean that ways of doing things are based on a large amount of common sense and compromise. Such arrangements may well be imperfect, but by codifying constitutional arrangements, it has always been held that the pay-off for codified 'clarity' is the handing of power from democratic institutions to the courts. The extent to which this is desirable in the UK is subject to intense debate.
- While the UK Supreme Court adopted the same title as its US namesake, the powers of the two bodies are incomparable. The US Supreme Court interprets the US constitution and determines whether laws — either at federal or state level — or actions of public officials are unconstitutional. If the US Supreme Court finds laws or actions to be in violation the US constitution, it has the power to strike them down.
- The UK Supreme Court has no such codified constitution to interpret. Consequently, the large majority of its workload lies in legal clarification, especially to establish whether actions of public officials and bodies or legislation is in breach of the law. The principle of parliamentary sovereignty means that the UK's constitutional arrangements are based substantially upon statute law, not on a codified constitution as in the USA. This means that judicial review in the UK has generally been less significant than in the USA, where US Supreme Court justices can strike down pieces of legislation which they deem to be contravening the US constitution.

Box 4.5 The role of the US Supreme Court

The US court is a product of a written, codified constitution from which it derives power even over Acts of Congress. The duty of the US Supreme Court to safeguard the Constitution and its Bill of Rights has taken it into controversial areas, such as abortion, which have been considered as much political as legal. Consequently, its prospective justices are subject to a high level of public and political scrutiny before appointment. Conversely, this type of public scrutiny is not part of the selection process for the UK Supreme Court.

Source: 'UK Supreme Court: ten years of treading the knife edge between politics and law' by Nicholas Clapham, 30 September 2019, https://theconversation.com

Summary

Ensure that you have a really effective grasp of a number of recent Supreme Court 'decided cases' across the range of its activity, especially those that highlight its role in protecting rights. In addition, be clear on the importance of the difference between judicial independence and judicial neutrality. The relationship between the branches is a central feature of the course, so evaluating the extent to which the judiciary can control and influence the executive branch is key. Other areas to consider:

- How are rights protected in the UK and to what extent is this the purpose of the judicial branch? How relevant is the Supreme Court ruling on parliament's prorogation to the protection of rights?
- The principles of judicial review and *ultra vires* are both important, so ensure that you have a range of examples for both aspects.
- How will withdrawal from the EU impact upon the power of the Court?

What next?

Read: Dr Maria Egan's article 'Ten years of the UK Supreme Court' in *Politics Review,* Volume 29, Issue 2

Watch: 'Supreme Court: Suspending Parliament was unlawful, judges rule' on YouTube

Research: the Institute for Government's articles on the Supreme Court, especially 'The Supreme Court has fortified Parliament's "constitutional role" — and its own' by Raphael Hogarth, 25 September 2019 available on **www.instituteforgovernment.org.uk**

Chapter 5

How 20 years of devolution have changed the UK and the challenges ahead

Exam success

Students require a thorough understanding of the process of devolution in the UK, including the roles and powers of the devolved bodies and the extent of the impact of devolved arrangements on the UK's multinational state. The best examination responses will demonstrate an effective grasp of all the key terms — such as 'nations', 'states', 'federalism', 'union' and 'unitary states' — and compare the contrasting theories of devolution with federalism. Top answers to the longer examination questions will analyse the advantages and disadvantages of devolution, incorporating recent examples of devolved power, and explain and evaluate the unresolved issues and the challenges that lie ahead. These arguments include the fact that the asymmetric, or dissimilar, process of devolution in the UK has had a destabilising impact upon the constitutional arrangements, and that England has been 'left behind', with neither a national assembly nor regional bodies to match those of Scotland, Wales and Northern Ireland.

Edexcel	UK Government 1.3	The role and powers of the devolved bodies in the UK, and the impact of this devolution on the UK
AQA	3.1.1.5	Devolution: ■ The roles, powers and responsibilities of the different devolved bodies in the UK ■ Impact of devolution on government of the UK

Context

Twenty years ago, the process of devolution was truly transformative for the United Kingdom. Wide-ranging powers, the control and management of public services and the ability to legislate in many areas of public life, were devolved from central government to bodies in Scotland, Wales and Northern Ireland. Newly formed regional institutions began to wield considerable power over the lives of their respective citizens.

Such arrangements appear now to be a permanent part of the UK's political and constitutional arrangements. But the relationship between devolved bodies and central government in Westminster is often regarded as anything but 'settled'. Over the last two decades, further powers have been transferred to the regions, often unevenly. Most recently, Brexit has added a whole new dimension of strain and uncertainty to the relationships between nations, with the diverging interest of the constituent parts of the UK laid bare.

Devolution has touched virtually every area of the UK's constitutional and political framework: from elections to party systems; taxation to public spending; healthcare provision, education and more. We have seen innovation, modernisation, and greater levels of democratic engagement, but also clashes over the distribution of power, disagreements over complex funding arrangements, and a perceived failure to fully consider how citizens in England are represented as effectively as those in the regions.

Box 5.1 Key definitions

Devolution in the UK: the process by which central government in Westminster delegates power to other levels of government. In the UK, the creation of devolved institutions in the regions 20 years ago saw a massive transfer of powers and responsibilities away from the centre. Devolved arrangements can have a degree of flexibility about the distribution of power, with responsibilities moving between regional and central governments without major constitutional upheaval.

Federalism: a form of government that sees power divided between central and regional authorities. Federal forms of government are often accompanied by highly entrenched constitutional arrangements, which clearly set out the relationships, responsibilities and spheres of influence. The USA operates a federal system with the central government in Washington responsible for economic, foreign and defence policies, and the states controlling most aspects of domestic and social policy.

How has the process of devolution developed since its origins?

There is no doubt that there have been many notable advantages of devolution in the last two decades. Policy decisions and spending priorities made within the regions are far more closely aligned to local needs. However, there are also rising concerns that public services controlled by the regions — especially health and education in some areas — are not thriving in the way that was envisioned. An article in *The Scotsman* (10 September 2019) reported the latest Scottish Household Survey, which found that satisfaction with the three public services — health, schools and public transport — was at its lowest level since the SNP came to power at Holyrood in 2007.

In addition, a substantial factor behind the process of devolution was a fear of the forces of nationalism and independence within the union. Consequently, for a full evaluation, account needs to be taken of the original devolution settlements and of the political backdrop against which the process of devolution has taken place.

The original devolution settlements were very different. From the outset, devolution differed substantially from one region to another.

- In **Scotland**, detailed planning had been underway since the mid-1980s with careful preparation and thought as to precisely what powers the new national institution would have. It was hardly surprising that almost 75% of Scots backed the devolved plans in the 1997 referendum.
- In **Wales**, plans and popular support were less developed that those of Scotland. In 1997, just 50.3% of Welsh people voted for an Assembly that, initially at least, had no power to pass its own primary legislation.
- In **Northern Ireland**, the process of devolution was inseparable from the peace process that had culminated in the ground-breaking Good Friday Agreement (1998). It was a self-governing deal that was very well supported in referendums that took place in both parts of Ireland.
- In **England**, devolution took the form of the creation of a London Assembly and a separately elected mayor. However, plans for regional devolution were halted when voters in the Northeast failed to support the creation of a regional government in a 2004 referendum.

For many commentators these initial differences are important, as they reflect the lack of a clear constitutional blueprint from the outset, a lack that has since destabilised the United Kingdom.

Box 5.2 Devolution — lacking a clear plan

In 2019, the Institute for Government stated that:

> There has been too little consideration of the future of the UK as a whole while devolution has advanced in different parts of the country. The lack of guiding principles has led to disagreement about the post-devolution constitution. Brexit has made it more urgent that governments and political parties address these big questions.

Source: www.instituteforgovernment.org.uk

The process of devolution has accompanied a decline in consensus politics in the UK. The 20 years between 1999 and 2019 have seen a significant change in the character of politics in the UK. The late 1990s was a period of broad alignment across the UK, largely under the New Labour umbrella. Since then:

- A Labour administration (1997–2010) has been replaced by a Conservative one (in coalition with the Liberal Democrats from 2010, and as a single-party government – with DUP support – from 2015) in Westminster.
- The Scottish Nationalist Party (SNP) has become the pre-eminent force in Scotland (see Table 5.1, and note that Scotland, like Wales, used the additional member electoral system or AMS) and its emphatic success in the December 2019 general election – gaining 13 seats to win 48 out of 59 constituercies – led to a fresh case for a second referendum being tabled.
- Northern Ireland politics has seen the more uncompromising wings of regional politics – the Democratic Unionist Party (DUP) and Sinn Féin – replace more moderate forces. This pattern continued in the 2019 general election, with the added dimension of the election of more nationalist MPs than unionist MPs for the first time in history.

- Wales has seen the Nationalist Party – Plaid Cymru – develop into a far more coherent political force, moving from zero seats at Westminster in 1970, to polling over 10% in the 2017 general election and securing four seats.

By 2019, the four regions of the UK were governed by at least as many different parties. The divergent agendas and priorities of these parties, magnified by prolonged cuts to public spending and by tensions caused by Brexit, have driven calls for even greater regional autonomy.

In response, and since 2011, there have been frequent changes to the devolution settlements as additional powers have been transferred. For example, while the Welsh Assembly was given full legislative powers in 2011, in 2016 Scotland gained greater taxation powers and control over social security.

Table 5.1 The rise of the Scottish National Party in regional elections

Year	Leader	Constituencies		Additional member		Total seats (out of 129)
		%	Seats (out of 73)	%	Seats (out of 56)	
1999	Alex Salmond	28.7	7	27.3	28	35
2003	John Swinney	23.7	9	20.9	18	27
2007	Alex Salmond	32.9	21	31.0	26	47
2011	Alex Salmond	45.4	53	44.0	16	69
2016	Nicola Sturgeon	46.5	59	41.7	4	63

What has the impact of 20 years of devolution been on UK politics?

While the process of devolution has made a lasting impression on many areas of the political, cultural, economic and constitutional life of the United Kingdom, two areas that are particularly relevant are the impact on elections and representation and on the process of government in the regions.

Elections and representation

After 20 years of devolution, there are now some major differences in party representation in the regions, caused in large part by the more proportional electoral systems used for regional elections.

- The most noticeable shifts have occurred in Scotland, where Labour's traditional regional strength (leading to single-party majority governments in the early years of devolution) has been supplanted by SNP-dominated or coalition governments. Labour fell to third behind the Scottish Conservatives in the 2016 general elections.
- In Wales, Labour has retained its strength, winning just under half of the assembly seats at each election of the last 20 years. Unlike the SNP, Plaid Cymru has yet to make a notable electoral breakthrough.
- In Northern Ireland, despite the main electoral winners being the more hard-line Democratic Unionists (DUP) and Sinn Fein at the expense of the Ulster Unionists and the Social Democratic and Labour Party, the region is the most multiparty of all, with four parties regularly securing more than a fifth of the seats each in devolved elections.

■ Turnout in regional elections tends to be lower than in general elections. While the aspiration of devolution was to bring representatives closer to the people, thereby making them more electorally sensitive, the average turnout in regional elections since 1999 is 52.3%, more than 10% lower than the 64% average for Westminster elections over the same period.

Governing the regions

One main objective of devolution was the aspiration to 'do politics differently'. On a practical level this meant that regional government was to be characterised far more by cross-party consensus-building, government by coalition and responsive, bottom-up policies. This aspiration has met with mixed success.

Table 5.2 Has devolution seen effective and innovative government over the last 20 years?

Yes	No
Regional legislatures have successfully enacted popular new laws in many different policy areas, several of which have influenced other regions or been adopted across the UK. • Scotland's 2006 ban on smoking in enclosed public places was adopted by other regions, then across the whole of the UK. • The Welsh administration introduced an 'opt-out' system for organ donation in 2015, coming into effect in England in 2020.	An important element of the original aspiration was to move away from the dominant executive model of the Westminster model. One measurement of the success of this is the proportion of successful bills introduced by the government compared to those introduced by ordinary assembly members (e.g. private Acts). During the 20 years of devolution, the Scottish and Welsh governments introduced 87% and 88% of the legislation respectively, both figures higher than that of 84% for government-backed legislation in Westminster.
The volume of primary legislation enacted by the regional governments reflects a healthy appetite for developing the regions in distinctive ways. In the last 20 years, Scotland has enacted almost 300 pieces of legislation: for an administration that did not exist until 1999, its legislative impact has been substantial.	The effectiveness of legislative scrutiny is open to question — there are far fewer regional members, and no regions have a second chamber. The Welsh Assembly in particular is widely considered to be too small to cope with the expanded powers recently afforded it. In Northern Ireland, power sharing has proved very difficult at times and the longest suspension — with powers reverting to the Northern Ireland Office — was for the whole of the Assembly's second term (October 2002–May 2007).

Yes	No
The power sharing agreement in Northern Ireland legally entrenches the requirement for coalitions to be formed that include representatives from parties on both sides of the community. Key votes in the Assembly require clearly stated proportions of support from both unionists and nationalists.	While the costs of running regional assemblies are less than running the UK Parliament, the costs per citizen are significantly higher (see Table 5.3), leading to questions over the value of extra levels of government during times of financial pressure.

Table 5.3 Costs of the devolved legislatures

	Total cost (£ million)	Cost per citizen per year (£)
UK Parliament	533	8.10
Scottish Parliament	99	18.25
Welsh Assembly	55	17.50
Northern Ireland Assembly	37	19.70

Source: HM Treasury

What challenges lie ahead for a devolved UK?

Most commentators conclude that devolution has been a qualified success over its first two decades. However, some of the main challenges ahead include:

1 **Repatriating EU powers:** the UK's withdrawal from the European Union has already been marked by disagreement and legal challenge to the way that EU powers will be returned to the UK. While some powers may naturally fall to devolved institutions (such as social security and aspects of taxation) others will not. The post-Brexit period will require a level of intergovernmental cooperation and trust that has not been seen during the process of the UK's withdrawal from the EU.

2 **Modernising funding arrangements:** the processes and formulas of funding for the regions remain highly complex, lack transparency and have been declared both unsuitable and undemocratic (see Box 5.3). Since different taxation powers have been devolved to different regions at different times and on different bases over the last 20 years, the complexities have magnified. An aspiration for greater accountability and financial transparency was part of the devolution process, yet funding devolution remains anything but.

Box 5.3 Funding the regions

The Barnett Formula was devised as a short-term measure by the then chief secretary to the Treasury Joel Barnett in the 1970s. In the absence of an agreed alternative, the formula was later adopted in the 1990s and is still used today. It uses a complex equation to adjust the levels of public finances allocated to the regions, depending on changes in spending in the rest of the UK. It is controversial because:

- It has no legal or democratic basis, existing only as a convention.
- It does not take account of needs or costs associated with each region.
- The House of Lords Select Committee on the Barnett Formula concluded 10 years ago in 2009 that 'the Barnett Formula should no longer be used to determine annual increases in the block grant for the United Kingdom's devolved administrations... A new system which allocates resources to the devolved administrations based on an explicit assessment of their relative needs should be introduced.' Yet it is still used today.

3 **Power-sharing in Northern Ireland:** while the measures that safeguard consensus in Northern Ireland are politically vital – not least because they were instrumental in garnering broad support for the original Good Friday Agreement – they have proved impractical at times, and insurmountable at others. Most recently, the collapse of power sharing from 2017 required substantial parliamentary legislation (the Northern Ireland Act, 2019) to ensure some degree of accountability during the period of direct rule from Westminster in the absence of a functioning Northern Ireland executive. However, the legitimacy of decisions taken about Northern Ireland's future remains in doubt.

4 **The future of England:** the story of devolution in the UK is the story of the non-English regions. There can be little doubt that England has been left substantially disadvantaged by the process of devolution, and any long-term settlement for Scotland, Wales and Northern Ireland needs to offer something similar – in terms of representation and responsive, engaged government – for England. The need for a mature and coherent debate over the future of England within the Union is impossible to ignore.

Table 5.4 Have 20 years of devolution been a success?

Yes	No
One of the main purposes of devolution was to calm the forces of nationalism. While 45% of voters in the 2014 Scottish referendum did indeed want independence, the UK remains united.	The union has only been preserved by further extensive powers being granted to the regions. Last ditch promises of ever more powers were considered to have swung the 2014 referendum.
Democracy and representation have both been enhanced through the creation of devolved assemblies and the use of more proportional electoral systems.	The practical performance of the regional bodies is in doubt, especially their capacity to cope with an expanding array of powers.
A much closer relationship between decisions, decision-makers and local needs has proved beneficial to the regions, and devolved institutions are popular.	The divergent political directions of the regions is placing a strain on relationships within the Union.
The UK's flexible constitution has accommodated the devolution of power from the centre to the regions.	The lack of a clear blueprint for the future of the UK has led to piecemeal changes and significant differences between the regions.

Parallels, connections and comparisons

- Scotland and Wales have both taken the initiative in enhancing democracy and voting rights — see chapter 7 on *Participation and voting rights* for analysis of the recent moves to lower the voting age to 16 and enfranchise prisoners. The devolution of oversight of elections has already led to different levels of engagement and enfranchisement within the United Kingdom.
- The process of devolution was a main component in New Labour's post-1997 constitutional reforms, aiming to democratise political decision-making in the UK. However, while the UK's flexible constitution has accommodated major changes, tensions within the Union appear to be growing rather than diminishing. Rather than calming calls for independence, in 2020, relationships appear to be more uncertain.
- Comparisons can easily be drawn between the fluidity of the UK's process of devolution and the rigidity of the federal arrangements in the USA. States in the USA may well be different, but they all have the same constitutionally entrenched law-making powers. In the UK, differences in the regions stem from the fact that they have different law-making powers, devolved from the centre on an ad hoc basis and at different times.

Summary

This chapter has provided an analysis of the process of devolution over the first 20 years of its lifespan, reviewing the strengths and weaknesses of the devolved institutions and arrangements, and the challenges that lie ahead. Other areas to review and debates to understand include:

- the origins and development of devolution in the UK, and the differences between federalism and devolution
- the composition and responsibilities of the devolved institutions and the extent to which they differ (asymmetric devolution) using specific examples of policy divergence
- the future of England, especially the prospects for an English national assembly or regional assemblies

What next?

Read:

Recent case studies of the regional governments can be found in *Politics Review*:

- a guide to devolved power in Wales, Volume 28, Issue 4
- a guide to devolved power in Scotland, Volume 29, Issue 2
- a guide to devolved power in Northern Ireland, Volume 29, Issue 4

Several useful resources have been produced by the Institute for Government (**www.instituteforgovernment.org.uk**) such as 'Devolution at 20', May 2019.

Chapter 6

Direct and representative democracy and recall elections strike in 2019

Exam success

Students aiming for the top grades need to be clear on the differences between direct democracy and representative democracy as well as being able to critically analyse and evaluate the advantages and disadvantages of each system. Effective understanding begins with the key features of democracy itself, and with some of the major principles upon which the A-level Politics course is based — those of accountability, legitimacy and consent.

Direct democracy in the UK usually comes in the form of referendums. Referendums are a controversial tool, and you should know why and how they have been used, and be able to back up answers with accurate recent examples. However, referendums are not the only example of direct democracy. While much has been written about the impact and influence of referendums recently, you need to be able to analyse and evaluate other important forms of direct involvement in the political process, especially the use of recall petitions in 2019, that look set to have an increasingly significant impact on this section of the A-level course.

Edexcel	UK Politics 1.1	Current systems of representative and direct democracy
AQA	3.1.2.1	Democracy and participation:
		■ Different types of democracy

Context

The 2009 parliamentary expenses scandal was a major shock to the UK's political system. There was widespread outrage at the disclosures relating to the misuse of the system of allowances and expenses available to Members of Parliament.

A legal challenge for the information to be made public, first under the Freedom of Information Act then through the courts, resulted in leaked details being published in the *Daily Telegraph* from May 2009. The revelations — which included extravagant claims for the furnishing of properties, over-claiming for food, avoiding tax on second home sales — dominated the media for many months, leading to public apologies, sackings, deselections and the early retirement of several MPs. A year later in 2010, criminal charges against four MPs led to their trials and imprisonment.

In the wake of the scandal, significant proposals for reforms to the UK's electoral and representative systems were tabled. The fact that MPs in the safest seats were twice as likely as those in the most marginal seats to be involved in the expenses scandal meant that mechanisms for removing (or 'recalling') MPs featured as part of these early proposals for reform.

Between 2010 and 2015 there was sustained support for recall elections to be introduced into the UK's political system. Arguments in their favour stressed that the mere possibility of a recall would serve to ensure that representatives would be far more attuned to their responsibilities — socially as well as politically. In a wider sense, their inception would play a part in restoring faith in the UK's system of representative democracy.

Box 6.1 Key definitions

Direct democracy: a system in which political decision are taken directly by the people. It is said to have originated in Ancient Athens when the city's citizens (approximately 40,000 men) were able to attend state meetings and vote on certain policies. In modern times, direct democracy usually takes the form of referendums in the UK. In some American states, such as in New England, regular direct involvement in the political decision-making remains a firm feature of local politics.

Representative democracy: sees citizens elect representatives to make political decisions on their behalf. This system of 'indirect democracy' is the basis for the UK's parliamentary democracy with MPs debating and voting on issues on behalf of the constituents who they represent. The modern form in the UK is often associated with the words of Edmund Burke who famously informed his Bristol constituents in 1774 that 'your representative owes you not his industry only but his judgement, and he betrays you if he sacrifices to your opinion'.

Why did recalls come to the UK in 2019?

In the wake of the MPs expenses scandal a raft of proposals were put forward in order to make MPs — even those in the safest seats — more responsive and accountable to their constituents. While the Representation of the People Act of 1981 required all MPs jailed for more than a year to give up their parliamentary seats, there were no mechanisms to force other MPs, such as those involved in 'scandals' or convicted of more minor offences, out of their seats except at the time of a general election.

Recall elections, along with the empowering of 'citizens justice', were not met with universal support. Opposition to the introduction of recalls focused upon the possibility that MPs might avoid locally unpopular decisions, that nevertheless might be in the national best interest, for fear of being 'recalled'. Indeed parliamentary debates on the bill sought assurances that MPs would not face recalls on the basis of their views. Other opponents of recalls raised the prospect that MPs would simply vote with their parties on an even more regular basis, for fear of being recalled by dissatisfied constituents if they did not.

In spite of sustained opposition, the Recall of MPs Act received Royal Assent in March 2015 and allows for the recall of an MP and the calling of a by-election. However, the Act states that a recall petition can only be issued by the speaker of the House of Commons, and only when an MP:

- has been convicted of an offence and receives a custodial prison sentence, or
- has been barred from the House of Commons for 10 sitting days or 14 calendar days, or
- has received a conviction for providing false or misleading expenses claims

This means that there are strict conditions under which a recall petition can be triggered. Importantly, and unlike in other countries, constituents themselves are unable to trigger a recall petition.

Box 6.2   What is a recall?

For a recall petition to be successful, 10% of eligible registered voters need to sign the petition. If the required number is not reached the petition fails and the MP remains in post. If the 10% threshold is reached, the petitions officer informs the speaker of the House of Commons that the recall petition has been successful. On the giving of that notice the seat becomes vacant. A by-election is then required and the recalled representative may stand as a candidate.

Source: www.parliament.uk

Box 6.3   Recalls in the USA

Recalls have been part of the American political system for nearly 400 years, with references to an elected body 'recalling' an official as early as 1631. However, more recently the process of recall has been codified into the constitutions of around one in three US states and refers to the ability of petitioners to trigger a special election following the identification of some form of malpractice in an office holder.

While the number of signatures required, and the timeframes to collect them, vary from state to state, the recall is a firm feature of modern American political culture.

- In 2003 the notable recall of Californian state governor Gray Davis was successful, and he was replaced in the subsequent special election by Arnold Schwarzenegger.
- In 2011 'peak recall' occurred when there were over 150 recall elections across the United States.
- In 2018 and 2019 the number of annual recalls settled back to single figures. In these years there were recalls for a range of elected officials including court judges, mayors and members of city councils.

What recall petitions have been made under the Act?

2018 saw the UK's first recall petition since the 2015 Act was passed into law. In July 2018, the Commons Select Committee on Standards recommended that Ian Paisley Jr., Member of Parliament for North Antrim since 2010, be suspended from the House of Commons for 30 sitting days for not declaring visits to Sri Lanka that were paid for by the Sri Lankan government.

However, in the prescribed 6-week period only 9.4% of the registered electorate signed the petition. Signatures totalled 7,099, almost 500 fewer than the requirement to reach 10% of the electorate in order to unseat the incumbent MP and force a by-election.

The Peterborough recall (March–May 2019)

The first successful recall petition occurred in Peterborough in 2019. Incumbent MP Fiona Onasanya was convicted of perverting the course of justice in early 2019, having misled the police in relation to their investigations over a speeding fine in 2017, and given a 3-month prison sentence. When her appeal against the conviction was rejected on 5 March 2019, Speaker of the House of Commons John Bercow announced on the same day that a recall petition would be put in place against her.

The petition ran from 19 March to 1 May 2019 and obtained 19,261 signatures — 27.6% of the 66,673 eligible electors, far exceeding the 10% required to vacate the seat.

The following month on 6 June, the first by-election took place as a result of a successful recall. It was won by Labour Party candidate Lisa Forbes with 30.9% (see Table 6.1), the lowest winning percentage of the vote in a by-election for over 70 years. In addition, turnout fell by almost 20% from 2017's general election constituency vote and the Labour Party candidate's winning margin was just 683 votes.

Table 6.1 Peterborough June 2019 by-election (candidates polling more than 1%)

Party	Candidate	Votes	%	% change
Labour	Lisa Forbes	10,484	30.91	−17.16
Brexit Party	Mike Greene	9,801	28.89	n/a
Conservative	Paul Bristow	7,243	21.35	−25.45
Liberal Democrat	Beki Sellick	4,159	12.26	+8.92
Green	Joseph Wells	1,035	3.05	+1.27
UKIP	John Whitby	400	1.18	n/a

The Brecon and Radnorshire recall (May–June 2019)

When Conservative MP Chris Davies pleaded guilty to charges of claiming false expenses in March 2019, he was sentenced to 50 hours of community work and given a £1,500 fine. His conviction triggered a recall petition under the 2015 Recall of MPs Act which was announced by the speaker of the House of Commons on 24 April 2019.

The recall petition ran from 9 May–20 June 2019 and, in spite of the Conservative Party officially registering to campaign for its failure, it collected almost double the required amount of signatures − 10,005 and 19% of the eligible electorate − and saw the removal of the incumbent MP.

In what was the first Westminster by-election to take place in August in nearly 40 years, the Conservative Party backed the convicted Chris Davies and saw Jane Dodds, the Liberal Democrat candidate, overturn the Conservative majority and take the seat with just over 43% of the vote (see Table 6.2). In patterns similar to the Peterborough by-election, turnout fell by over 17% from 2017's general election constituency vote.

Table 6.2 August 2019 Brecon and Radnorshire by-election (all candidates)

Party	Candidate	Votes	%	% change
Liberal Democrat	Jane Dodds	13,826	43.46	+14.36
Conservative	Christopher Davies	12,401	38.98	−9.62
Brexit Party	Des Parkinson	3,331	10.47	n/a
Labour	Tom Davies	1,680	5.28	−12.42
Monster Raving Loony	Lady Lily the Pink	334	1.05	n/a
UKIP	Liz Phillips	242	0.76	−0.64

Have recalls enhanced democracy in the UK?

Problems associated with the UK's representative democracy are well documented. The majoritarian electoral system routinely produces unrepresentative outcomes. A high proportion of constituency seats are considered to be safe, with around two-thirds rarely changing hands from one general election to another. Five-year gaps between general elections can make governments and individual MPs complacent, unresponsive and unaccountable. Consequently, the 2015 Recall of MPs Act was seen by many as a victory for citizens over the political establishment.

Table 6.3 Have recalls enhanced democracy in the UK?

Yes	No
Recalls improve accountability and empower citizens. There is little doubt that the right to recall has significantly enhanced the accountability of elected officials. In the fight to halt the decline of trust in politicians in the wake of the expenses scandal, this is a tool which gives citizens a significant sanction against representatives engaged in misconduct.	Recalls have further polarised politics. While the triggering of a recall petition may be subject to strict legal criteria, the aftermath of a successful petition has seen even greater political polarisation and division. Campaigning tactics in the Brecon and Radnorshire by-election led to a pro-Remain pact which saw candidates for the Green Party and Plaid Cymru stand aside to allow for votes to be concentrated on the Liberal Democrats. The tactic denied voters a proper democratic choice and reduced the election to the 'debate of the day': Brexit.
They counter the forces of populism. The flames of populism are often fanned by conspiracy theories, misplaced suspicion and baseless accusations. The anti-establishment, 'anti-corruption', stances of many populists are undermined by the advent of recall petitions which have provided a formal basis for the recalling of a representative, thereby exposing mischievous and baseless demands for representatives to face unspecified consequences.	They trigger by-elections which are notoriously unrepresentative. The results of by-elections in the UK have long been subject to forces at odds with the predominantly consensual currents of politics in the UK. The Peterborough by-election saw the Brexit Party — a single-issue political party formed just a few months earlier — come second, less than 2% behind the winner. Governing parties usually receive a trouncing in by-elections and 2019 was no exception, with the Conservative vote falling by over 25% in Peterborough and by nearly 10% in Brecon and Radnorshire.
There are significant safeguards. Some early opponents of recalls pointed to the 'chaos' of the widespread use of recalls across the USA in 2011. However, the crucial difference between the UK and USA is that recall procedures in many American states can be triggered by citizens themselves, allowing highly mobilised special interest groups to succeed in unseating political opponents. Under the 2015 Act in the UK, only the speaker can trigger a recall petition, and only under strict circumstances.	They do not go far enough. Currently, the mechanism to trigger a recall petition is (a) in the hands of the speaker of the House of Commons, and (b) focused almost exclusively upon 'corruption'. A recent petition from 38 Degrees has instead called for a 'real' recall, encouraging citizens to 'support a recall bill that puts the power in voters hands, so that if, in between general elections, enough voters were dissatisfied enough with their MP to petition for a by-election, they could do so'.

The most vocal campaigner for extending the right of recall when the bill was being debated in the Commons was the then Conservative MP Zac Goldsmith. Goldsmith argued that if 20% of voters sign a petition, an MP should be 'sacked' and a by-election held. However, for many others, the restrictions placed on the triggering of the recall process cut an appropriate line between ensuring that MPs convicted of serious offences can be removed while ensuring that the process cannot be hijacked by powerful pressure groups or malicious media campaigns.

Parallels, connections and comparisons

- Many of the arguments concerning recall petitions echo those relating to democracy and direct democracy. Just like referendums, recall petitions are a feature of direct democracy at odds with the UK's system of representative democracy. The representative process seeks to thwart an inherent weakness of democracy — the tyranny of the majority. But should the right to recall be extended further, the move would be considered by many to be anti-democratic, making elected representatives overly fearful of upsetting their constituents.
- Debates about recall elections and democracy also touch upon the key thinkers. Edmund Burke has been referenced above, and in *On Liberty* (1859), John Stuart Mill expressed similar caution over the way in which democracy could be subverted by a mobilised 'majority' that forces its will over a minority. Such a state of affairs, argued Mill, is more comparable to authoritarian regimes than democratic ones.
- In the USA, recall elections are part of a raft of political procedures that permit citizens to be directly involved in the decision-making process. Comparisons can be made between recalls in the UK and USA but only up to a point. Unlike the UK, many American states permit recalls to be initiated by voters themselves, and their extent is substantially different. Recalls in the USA are far more frequent: 26 separate recalls were held on 8 November 2011 alone, and at any one time there can be over 20 recall efforts underway — see Ballotpedia (ballotpedia.org) for the latest recall efforts.

Summary

The advantages and disadvantages of direct democracy and representative democracy and the case for reform the UK's systems are prominent parts of the A-level specifications. Evaluating the state of democracy in the UK is also significant. Referring to whether the UK remains a pluralist democracy is part of this debate — whether power and influence are widely dispersed and whether different views and opinions are tolerated.

What next?

- **Read:** the related article 'Are referendums the best form of democracy?' by Nick Gallop in *Politics Review*, Volume 29, Issue 1
- **Watch:** some interesting debates and perspectives expressed during the passage of the 2015 Recall Bill. Discussions from the Political and Constitutional Reform Committee can be found here: **https://publications. parliament.uk/pa/cm201213/cmselect/cmpolcon/373/373.pdf**

Chapter 7

Participation and voting rights: extending the franchise

Exam success

Understanding the issues and debates surrounding the franchise — the right to vote — is a central requirement of the examination specifications. For students following the Edexcel specification, the focus is on debates over a 'wider' franchise, the nature of suffrage and on evaluating the work of a current movement to further extend voting rights. For students following the AQA specification, the focus is similarly on the nature and scope of the franchise, with debates centring on the extent to which suffrage should be considered a human right. Consequently, the best candidates will be able to analyse and evaluate the most recent developments in the widening of the franchise and to link these coherently to the nature of the UK's democracy and the enhancement of political participation in the UK.

Edexcel	UK Politics 1.2	A wider franchise and debates over suffrage: ■ The work of a current movement to extend the franchise
AQA	3.1.2.1	Democracy and participation: ■ How suffrage has changed since the Great Reform Act to the present ■ Suffrage as a human right

Context

There are three main debates concerning the extension of the franchise in the UK, namely:

■ Should the voting age be lowered to 16?
■ Should prisoners continue to be denied the right to vote?
■ Should voting be made compulsory?

2019 saw significant and potentially momentous developments in two of these long-standing challenges: the extension of the franchise to 16- and 17-year-olds and the enfranchisement of prisoners.

Students will study numerous examples of the ways in which citizens can participate in the political process. These include joining parties, active membership of pressure groups, and the signing of local or national petitions and e-petitions. However, by far the most significant method of political participation is voting, especially voting in general elections, as the level of turnout at a general election is a key indicator of both the democratic health of a state and the legitimacy of the elected assembly itself. Consequently, denying certain groups the right to participate in elections is a highly contentious issue.

The campaign to enfranchise 16- and 17-year-olds was boosted substantially by the inclusion of 16- and 17-year-olds in the electorate just prior to the Scottish independence referendum in 2014. More than 109,000 of the 3.6 million referendum voters were below the age of 18. 16- and 17-year-olds are now eligible to vote in Scottish Parliamentary and local elections too. The campaign to enfranchise this younger group of voters intensified in 2019, as Wales followed Scotland's lead in introducing legislation.

In August 2019, the Scottish government announced that prisoners serving a sentence of less than 12 months would get the right to vote on a temporary basis under new legislation. Denying prisoners the right to vote has been a particularly contentious issue ever since the European Court of Human Rights ruled in 2005 that the UK's blanket ban on prisoners' voting is unlawful. Campaign groups like the Prison Reform Trust have long highlighted the fact that there are few (or no) votes in prison reform and little interest in the rights and responsibilities of those behind bars. One of the reasons is that prisoners themselves cannot vote.

Box 7.1 Key definitions

Suffrage: the right to vote, also known as the franchise. Almost all adult citizens in the UK have the right to vote — universal suffrage. However, with a prison population of over 80,000, prisoners represent the largest single disenfranchised adult group in the UK.

Turnout: the percentage of registered voters who cast a vote at an election. Turnout in postwar general elections averaged over 75% but fell to an average of below 62% for the three general elections between 2001 and 2010. The higher level of turnout in 2015 (66.1%), 2017 (68.7%) and 2019 (67.3%) has provided some reassurance that representative democracy in the UK remains healthy.

Should the voting age be lowered to 16?

For democracies to function effectively, an active and engaged citizenry is essential. An argument often forwarded is that by engaging young people in politics in their formative years, future democratic health is likely to be enhanced.

The Electoral Reform Society (ERS) is currently a key campaigner for the extension of the right to vote to 16- and 17-year-olds. The ERS asserts that where they are currently eligible to vote, voters in this youngest group have higher rates of turnout than 18- to 24-years olds (see Box 7.2). The Electoral Reform Society is a founding member of the Votes at 16 coalition. This coalition involves the Scottish National Party (SNP), the Labour Party, the Liberal Democrats and the Greens, who all support votes at 16.

During the debate, academics asserted that of 47 Council of Europe members, only the UK, Armenia, Bulgaria, Estonia and Russia denied prisoners the vote.

The matter was passed to the Local Government and Communities Committee which consulted on the matter and reported in June 2019. The committee could not find consensus, but recommended that prisoners serving sentences of 4 years or less should be entitled to register to vote in Assembly elections. However, the Welsh Assembly has yet to legislate to enfranchise prisoners.

> **Box 7.6** **Divisions over the enfranchisement of prisoners in the Welsh Assembly**
>
> The move to enfranchise prisoners was not universally supported. Welsh Conservative Mark Isherwood said: 'Plaid Cymru say they are holding this to enhance the human rights of prisoners: but what about the human rights of victims that were violated by murderers, terrorists, rapists, and paedophiles?'
>
> In response, Plaid Cymru representative Leanne Wood said: 'Denying a whole group of people the right to have their say on decisions which affect them cannot be justified in a modern, democratic society.'

Developments in England

In 2017 David Liddington, the then justice secretary, circulated proposals to ministers that prisoners sentenced to less than a year in jail and who are let out on day release would be allowed to return home to vote. The plans were met with significant opposition from Conservative ranks, with reactions against the ECtHR's decision in 2005.

Philip Davies, the Conservative MP for Shipley, said:

> I am wholly opposed to it. I am against giving prisoners the vote. Prisoners released on temporary licence are still prisoners. I don't recognise the validity of the court's decision. The court has made a mistake here, not the government. Whether prisoners should have the vote is a matter that should be decided by a democratically elected Parliament.

However, Diane Abbott, the then shadow home secretary, told BBC One's *Andrew Marr Show* that Labour backed the stance of the European Court of Human Rights. Diane Abbott said:

> The European Court of Human Rights has been saying for some years that we can't stop all prisoners having the vote and the Labour Party believes that we should indeed, in the end, we have to support the position of the European Court of Human Rights.

Since then here have been no further moves to enfranchise prisoners in elections that take place in England.

Parallels, connections and comparisons

- The information contained in this chapter is valuable for studies of civil liberties groups too. There are some good examples within it of notable groups campaigning for the rights of minority or disenfranchised groups, a key component of the work of civil liberty pressure groups.
- There are also notable connections with the devolution topic. The organisation of elections is a responsibility for devolved governments in the UK and consequently electoral rules (along with electoral systems) vary significantly between the regions, with Scotland being the first region to enfranchise 16-year-olds.
- Additionally, similar debates about the enfranchisement of prisoners are taking place in the USA. Many Democratic contenders for the party's presidential nomination have made bold statements to enfranchise prisoners. Prominent campaigners, such as Bernie Sanders, and well-organised interest groups, such as Florida Rights Restoration Coalition, have pledged major reforms to prisoners' voting rights.

Summary

The debate on extending the franchise — whether lowering the age rate to 16 or widening it to include prisoners — is part of a far broader discussion on the nature of participation, representation, democracy and legitimacy in the UK. Knowledge of the developments in widening the right to vote in the UK is an important requirement of the course, and the information in this chapter relates to wider debates which include:

- an evaluation of the merits of the UK's representative democracy
- the issues surrounding the current state of the franchise in the UK, whether based on gender, age, ethnicity or socioeconomic status
- how political participation might be enhanced in the UK

What next?

- **Listen:** 'Let's Raise the Voting Age', an alternative angle on the debate on the voting age hosted by Professor James Tilley on Radio 4, can be found on BBC iPlayer (**www.bbc.co.uk/programmes**)
- **Watch:** the futuristic television series, *Black Mirror*. In the third and final episode of the second series, Waldo, a blue cartoon bear, contests a by-election and comes close to derailing normal democratic politics
- **Read:** the Welsh Assembly's 2019 research report 'Extending the franchise: prisoner voting' available on **https://gov.wales**

Chapter 8

Pressure groups and civil liberties in 2019

Exam success

Pressure groups, particularly those focused on civil liberties or seeking to extend the franchise, feature in several areas of the examination specifications, notably in the specific sections on pressure groups themselves, with a focus upon varying influence and methods. The most successful pressure groups employ a wide array of tactics, ranging from submissions to Parliament to e-petitions to organised civil disobedience. The best responses will be able to explain the range of methods within the context of what constitutes 'success' — depending on original aims and objectives. Top responses will be able to utilise contemporary examples, especially those that relate to new technologies and aspects of censorship and surveillance to evaluate the changing nature of pressure group activity.

Edexcel	UK Politics 1.3	Pressure groups and other influences: ■ How different pressure groups exert influence and how their methods vary in contemporary politics ■ Case studies of two different pressure groups, highlighting examples of how their methods and influence vary
	UK Politics 1.4	Rights in context: ■ Debates on the extent, limits and tensions within the UK's rights-based culture, including consideration of how individual and collective right may conflict
AQA	3.1.1.1	The nature and sources of the British Constitution: ■ Debates about the extent of rights in the UK
	3.1.2.4	Pressure groups: ■ Methods used by pressure groups

Context

New forms of media, information and communication technology have undoubtedly transformed the way that people interact — with each other and with the state. Online activity can have great benefits in underpinning pluralist democracies. It can encourage mass participation and engagement, promote informed debate, boost e-petitions, crowdfund new ventures, and expose all manner of activities that those in authority might prefer members of the public to remain unaware of. However, it can also promote abuse, bullying, intimidation, and the proliferation of fake news and disinformation. One central question is who controls the internet? And in whose name should censorship — if at all — be carried out?

2019 saw the continued roll-out of several technological threats to privacy and civil liberties — notably the spread of facial recognition technology in public spaces, concerns over censorship of social media platforms and the escalation of police powers to digitally 'strip search' the technology (mobile phones and other devices) of people under investigation. Several notable groups have come to increasing prominence as they draw attention to the threats that the misuse — or misapplication — of technology can bring.

Box 8.1 Key definitions

Pressure groups: organised usually single-issue groups of people who share the same sectional interests or causes. Their aim is to work in a coordinated way to further their interests — mainly by raising awareness of their issues or by pressuring decision-makers into promoting favourable legislation.

Pluralist democracy: a system of government that encourages participation and civic engagement and promotes the proliferation of different ideas, opinions and political views. For pluralism to thrive, there needs to be multiple centres of power beyond the state — independent political parties, business groups, education systems and other organisations.

Privacy, censorship and surveillance

Web tracking, data collection, the interconnection of smart domestic devices (which may well be unsecure and sending large amounts of personal information to third parties), public Wi-Fi, social media snooping — are all prevalent factors in our ever-growing dependency on technology to keep us interested, engaged, healthy or safe.

However, the technological threat to our privacy and liberty has become a preoccupation of several of the more prominent pressure groups. Consequently, many governmental groups and organisations in many different countries are coming to the conclusion that mass surveillance practices are a fundamental threat to human rights, violating the right to privacy that is enshrined in the laws of most states.

Liberty and facial recognition software

Liberty is one of the UK's oldest civil liberty groups, campaigning since 1934. Its stated aims are to challenge injustice, defend freedom, and to work to make sure that the UK becomes a fairer society.

One of the biggest ongoing campaigns of Liberty is to resist the proliferation of facial recognition software used in an increasing number of public places, such as shopping centres and stations. The technology can photograph individuals and create biometric maps of their faces that, says the group, 'are then compared to images on secretive watchlists'. Liberty also claims that at least one police force 'has plans to start using the tech on officers' mobile phones, making it easier for them to scan us on the move'.

Liberty's aim is for a complete ban on the use of facial recognition technology by police and by private companies in publicly accessible places. Not only that, but Liberty claims there is a more insidious agenda: that police are targeting locations with predominantly black, Asian and minority ethnic or working-class populations which is 'embedding discriminatory approaches to policing'.

One of Liberty's main methods is to raise awareness of the issue through its website and the use of social media with the reinforcement of four key messages:
- Facial recognition violates everyone's privacy: biometric data is scanned without consent, contributing to a level of surveillance that 'breaches our right to privacy'.
- Facial recognition makes us change our behaviour: Liberty explains that when they know they are being watched, people alter where they go and what they do.
- Facial recognition is discriminatory: Liberty claims that the 'technology discriminates against people of colour and women', meaning they are 'more likely to be misidentified and stopped by the police'.
- Facial recognition has no place on our streets: MPs from all parties have joined the campaign to force a suspension in facial recognition deployments.

As well as raising awareness of the issue, Liberty is pursuing two main methods.

Method 1: A public petition
A petition to ban facial recognition software 'in places like shopping centres and train stations' was addressed to the home secretary. By early November 2019 it had achieved the required 10,000 signatures needed to get a response from the government.

Method 2: Through the courts
South Wales Police was one of the first police forces in the UK to adopt automated facial recognition software, first using it during the Champions League final in Cardiff in May 2017. It has been used at major events since.

In May 2019, a man who was photographed while shopping in Cardiff took South Wales Police to court claiming that the use of technology on him was an unlawful violation of this privacy.

However, on 4 September 2019, the High Court found the use of automated facial recognition software by South Wales Police to be 'lawful'. A Liberty lawyer stated that: '... this disappointing judgment does not reflect the very serious threat that facial recognition poses to our rights and freedoms'.

To find out more on Liberty's campaign go to **www.libertyhumanrights.org.uk/resist-facial-recognition**.

Privacy International and advertising transparency
Privacy International (PI) is an independent charity that challenges governments and companies 'that want to know everything about individuals, groups and

whole societies'. Formed in 1990, PI is active all over the world and campaigns against threats to personal privacy.

A current PI campaign concerns advertising transparency. PI seeks to highlight the role of social media and search platforms in political campaigning and elections, highlighting the:

- spread of disinformation
- profiling of users without their knowledge
- micro-targeting of users with tailored messages
- interference by foreign entities

Method 1: Raising awareness by lobbying bodies such as the European Commission

There has been greater attention paid to the transparency of political advertisements in recent years (see Box 8.2). In 2019, Privacy International focused its attention on the European Commission which was regulating the extent to which companies are adhering to the Code of Practice on Disinformation. The Commission's report on the code can be found on **https://ec.europa.eu/digital-single-market/en/news/code-practice-disinformation**.

Box 8.2 Excerpt from the European Commission's Code of Practice

This is the first time worldwide that industry agrees, on a voluntary basis, to self-regulatory standards to fight disinformation. The Code aims to achieve the objectives set out by the Commission's Communication presented in April 2018 by setting a wide range of commitments, from transparency in political advertising to the closure of fake accounts and demonetisation of purveyors of disinformation.

The Code of Practice was signed by the online platforms Facebook, Google and Twitter, Mozilla, as well as by advertisers and advertising industry in October 2018, and signatories presented their roadmaps to implement the Code. In May 2019, Microsoft subscribed to the Code of Practice and also presented its roadmap.

Source: European Commission's 'Digital single market' papers

Box 8.3 Privacy International: empowering people with advertising transparency

In the lead-up to the 2019 EU Parliamentary elections Facebook, Google, and Twitter, as well as the Interactive Advertising Bureau and others, agreed to take a series of steps to prevent online disinformation on their respective platforms. These measures are reflected in a self-regulatory Code of Practice on Disinformation and the companies provided the European Commission with monthly updates on their progress.

The European Commission reported on the extent to which companies met their commitments in November 2019. Prior to this, Privacy International had already highlighted its findings that companies only adopt the self-regulatory practices where there are regulatory pressures. And in particular some companies approaches are notably fragmented:

- Facebook provides heightened transparency for political advertisements in 35 countries (roughly 17% of the countries in the world). This means that for roughly 83% of the countries in the world, the company does not require political advertisers to become authorised, for political advertisements to carry disclosures, or for advertisements to be archived.
- Google provides heightened transparency for political advertisements in 30 countries (roughly 15% of the countries in the world).
- Twitter provides heightened transparency for advertisements tied to specific elections (rather than political advertisements more generally) in 32 countries (roughly 16% of the countries in the world).

Method 2: Submissions to the UK Parliament

In September 2019, Privacy International made a submission the UK Parliament's House of Lords Committee on Democracy and Digital Technologies. Highlighting concerns that democratic participation can be inhibited by surveillance – both by governments and private companies – PI launched its campaign Defending Democracy and Dissent, which aims to investigate the role technology plays in facilitating and/or hindering everyone's participation in civic society.

This submission aimed to provide information to the House of Lords committee, covering a range of aspects such as:

- how digital technology has changed the way democracy works
- the need for greater transparency and accountability in online spending and campaigning of political groups
- the effect of online advertising on the political process
- risks that social media undermines the trust in the democratic process and what should be done

Find out more by visiting **https://privacyinternational.org**.

Big Brother Watch and challenging the surveillance state

Big Brother Watch styles itself as a cross–party, independent organisation leading the protection of privacy and civil liberties in the UK. It seeks to expose and challenge threats to privacy, freedom and civil liberties at a time of enormous technological change in the UK.

Big Brother Watch campaigns through parliamentary lobbying and through the courts. It produces unique research and conducts independent investigations and seeks to educate and empower the public.

Method 1: Challenging adverse parliamentary legislation

In 2019 there were two bills in parliament, introduced by Labour MPs attempting to require online forum administrators and moderators to remove content that has been deemed harmful and damaging. The bills were:

- The Online Forums Bill, which was introduced in 2018 as a Private Member's bill by Lucy Powell. The bill stated that 'those with malign intent are able to exploit the openness of social media to spread hate and disinformation' and that this 'misuse of social media' requires legislation to address it. Big Brother Watch released a briefing paper to oppose the bill claiming that it posed a threat 'to people's privacy, freedoms and civil liberties at a time of enormous technological change in the UK'.
- The Social Media Service Providers (Civil Liability and Oversight) Bill sought to place limits on the internet's capacity for 'lasting harm' and to tackle the 'erosion of trust that the internet and new technologies' have had. Big Brother Watch produced a briefing paper explaining that in requiring (profit-driven) social media companies to remove content, it would have 'a significant effect on people's fundamental rights to free expression and privacy online'.

Both bills have yet to progress past the first reading stage. The opposition of free speech groups such as Big Brother Watch, who explained what the unintended consequences could be of greater web censorship on the part of social media companies, was seen as a substantial check to their progress.

Method 2: Using mainstream media to raise awareness

Spokespeople from Big Brother Watch have appeared on a number of prominent and mainstream news and talk shows to highlight relevant issues and raise awareness:

- In 2 months alone — over August and September 2019 — the group appeared on several notable news programmes and channels such as the BBC news, ITV news, Channel 5 News, Al Jazeera, ABC news in America, and HuffPost to debate and discuss technological threats to liberty and privacy such as:
  - the use of facial recognition software
  - 'digital strip searches' and the methods that police use to obtain digital evidence in their investigations
  - the use that local councils make of CCTV footage
- The group produces and distributes several press releases each month, notably on government threats to online privacy, facial recognition software and the digital privacy of victims during police investigations.

Find out more by visiting **https://bigbrotherwatch.org.uk**.

Parallels, connections and comparisons

- Conflict between liberty and security is a permanent feature of modern democratic states. States are often walking a tightrope between regulation that seeks to protect individuals and the state, and excessively restrictive or discriminatory laws that stifle individual freedom. The usual conflicted territory can be seen as being between:
  - freedom of expression versus the rights of groups not to have their faith or beliefs ridiculed
  - press freedom versus the right of public figures to private lives
  - the right to demonstrate peacefully versus the right of communities to be free from nuisance

- The rising level of surveillance is a p██████████████████
  globe. London is regularly listed as bei████████████████
  to numbers of CCTV cameras, with a total o████████
  9,176,530 people (just over 68 cameras for ever█████
  CCTV-heavy city in the world is Shanghai in China █████
  in 2019.
- Pressure groups in the US have long enjoyed a privileged p████
  political system. A codified constitution provides clarity on wh██
  can be championed and which are potentially being infringed; and ██
  access points — either at federal or state level or between the separate██
  branches of government (president, Supreme Court and Congress) — along██
  with the frequency and regularity of election cycles means that methods
  and targets for influence are numerous.

Summary

Pressure groups are permanent features of modern democratic states: able
to challenge the government and hold to account decision-makers as well
as to push for the interests of the sections of society that they represent.
The extent to which technology furthers group ends — or indeed whether it
becomes the target of pressure group activity itself, as seen in this chapter —
needs to be balanced against other requirements of the topic. Consider also:

- the range of pressure group methods and how these might affect success
- whether technological changes, or the advent of digital democracy,
  necessitates a revaluation of classifications of pressure groups to
  understand why some types of groups are more successful than others

What next?

Read:

- 'Is facial recognition technology working for South Wales Police and what
  happens when it goes wrong?' on the WalesOnline website:
  www.walesonline.co.uk
- Privacy International's Research Paper: 'Social media companies have failed
  to provide adequate advertising transparency to users globally' on Privacy
  International's website: **https://privacyinternational.org**

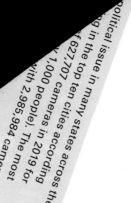

...election
...n of first

...eatures of the first-past-the-
...ntages and disadvantages
...and decisiveness, with its
...y that it regularly marginalises all
...P to create large numbers of safe
...is ever realistically likely to win,
...fuels calls for its replacement with
a mc...

Success in the ...igh level of understanding of at least
one alternative electo... ...er to discuss benefits and drawbacks
in comparison with FPTP. Son... ...ms used in non-Westminster elections
in the UK are not proportional, such as the supplementary vote (SV) used
for many mayoral election, while others are highly proportional, such as
the single transferable vote (STV) used in Northern Ireland. The additional
member system (AMS), used in Scotland and Wales, combines aspects of
both. Exam success also requires candidates to provide detailed evidence of
elections from before and after 1997.

| Edexcel | UK Politics 3.1–3.3 | Electoral systems |
| AQA | 3.1.2.2 | Elections and referendums |

Context

Political and parliamentary systems are largely based upon the effects of
the electoral systems that are used to create them. In this regard, the UK's
Westminster Parliament is the product of a majoritarian electoral system that
does not translate votes to seats accurately but that does (more often than
not) create stable, single-party governments.

The strengths of first past the post were well evidenced in a postwar period
that saw all but one of the general elections between 1945 and 2010 result in
the creation of a single-party government. Since then, in the three elections
between 2010 and 2017, FPTP successively led to the creation of a coalition
government (in 2010), a government with one of the smallest postwar
majorities of just 12 seats (in 2015), and a minority government (in 2017).

The 2019 general election bucked this recent trend and the Conservative Party secured the largest working government majority since the 2001 election. That said, the disparity between seats won and votes cast is arguably as stark as ever, with the Conservatives securing a majority of 80 seats in parliament (56% of the seats in the House of Commons) based on less than 44% of the votes cast. Needless to say, the 2019 result reignited arguments over the extent to which the strengths of first past the post outweigh its weaknesses.

Box 9.1 Key definitions

First past the post: the electoral system used for Westminster elections. It relies on candidates in single-member constituencies winning a simple plurality, just one more vote than their nearest constituency rival. The nature of constituency-based voting means that large numbers of votes are 'wasted'.

Proportional representation: describes electoral systems with a close alignment between votes cast and seats won. A large number of electoral systems, that are proportional or that have an element of proportionality, are used in the UK for non-Westminster elections. These include:

- **Additional member system (AMS):** a hybrid of FPTP and the regional party list system, used for elections to the devolved assemblies of Scotland and Wales.
- **Single transferable vote (STV):** a highly proportional system, used for elections to the Northern Ireland Assembly.

Top ten takeaways from the 2019 general election

1 Victory for the **Conservative Party** gave it the largest governing majority since Labour's second landslide win in 2001. The headlines of the 2019 general election were the record-equalling fourth successive general election victory enjoyed by the Tories, their 47-seat gain, and their Commons majority of 80 seats. The number of votes cast for the Conservatives was 13,966,565, higher even than the number secured by Tony Blair in 1997 (13,518,167).

2 The **Labour Party** experienced an emphatic defeat. The odds should have been stacked in favour of the Opposition, but Labour lost 59 seats and its share of the vote declined by 7.9% from 40% in 2017 to 32.2% in 2019. In securing just 202 seats, it was Labour's worst postwar general election performance. The reasons behind the Labour Party's defeat are developed in Chapter 10.

3 The story of 2019 was also one of heavy defeat for the **Liberal Democrats**. Despite receiving almost 3.7 million votes (up 4.2% on 2017) and 11.6% of the total votes cast, the party lost 13 seats (9 of these had been gained since the 2017 election due to several MPs moving to the Liberal Democrats) and gained just 3. Overall, they had one less seat than from the result of the 2017 election. The Liberal Democrat leader Jo Swinson lost her own seat of Dunbartonshire East and stepped down as party leader.

4 Historic **new voting patterns** were established in 2019, most notably the transfer of support from long-standing Labour constituencies in the so-called 'red wall', the solid band of Labour-held seats across the Midlands and North, many of which have been returning successive Labour Party MPs for generations.

5 Despite there never having been a December general election in the postwar period, **turnout** at the damp and chilly 2019 vote was reassuringly in line with previous elections. A turnout figure of 67.3% in 2019 was far closer to the recent high of 71.4% in 1997, than the recent low of 59.4% in 2001.

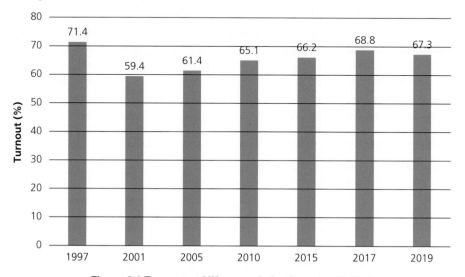

Figure 9.1 Turnout at UK general elections, 1997–2019

6 **Scotland** saw a reassertion of the pre-eminence of the Scottish National Party. The SNP had slipped back from former highs to secure 35 of the 59 Scottish constituency seats in 2017. In 2019 however, they returned 48 MPs (winning over 80% of Scottish constituencies) from 45% of the Scottish vote. First past the post played out well for the SNP. Its 1,242,380 votes resulted in 48 MPs, but the combined total of Conservative and Labour votes (1,204,777) secured them just 7 seats (6 and 1 respectively). See Table 9.1.

Table 9.1 2019: the result in Scotland

Party	Seats (change)	2019 vote share (%)	Share change	2019 votes	Vote change
SNP	48 (+13)	45	+8.1	1,242,380	+246,811
Conservatives	6 (–7)	25.1	–3.5	692,939	–65,010
Liberal Democrats	4 (=)	9.5	+2.8	263,417	+84,356
Labour	1 (–6)	18.6	–8.5	511,838	–205,169

7 Elsewhere in the UK, outcomes were similarly noteworthy. In **Wales**, Labour's vote share fell by 8% and the party returned 22 MPs, 6 fewer than 2017's result. However, with a relatively small change in its total vote share (up 2.5% to 36.1%) the Conservative Party won 6 more seats to return 14 MPs from Welsh constituencies. In **Northern Ireland**, the Democratic Unionist Party (DUP) lost 2 seats to the Social Democratic and Labour Party (SDLP) meaning that from 2019, nationalists and republican parties have a greater number of Westminster MPs.

8 Following the 2019 votes, the House of Commons was heralded as the most diverse ever with record numbers of **women and ethnic minority representatives** returned. While almost two thirds of MPs remain male, a record 220 MPs (34%) are women. There remain stark differences between the parties – just 87 of the 365 Tory MPs are female, whist over half (104 of 202) Labour MPs are female. MPs from ethnic minority backgrounds also rose in number from 52 to 63 – to almost 10% of MPs.

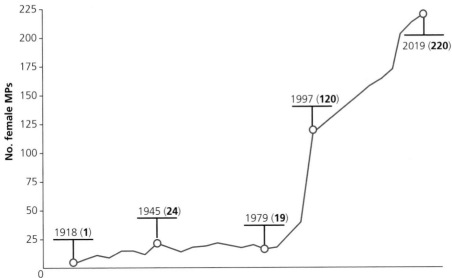

Figure 9.2 Number of female MPs elected at UK general elections, 1918–2019

9 The pre-election **opinion polls** were accurate. The majority of the polling companies' individual polls were broadly similar to the final result and the largest news websites, e.g. Sky News, BBC, Guardian online, ran 'poll of polls' that converged within 1% of each other and the final result. The BBC's poll tracker underpredicted Conservative support by 1% and overpredicted Labour support by 1%. The final polls published by Opinium and Ipsos Mori were almost spot on.

10 Was 2019 the '**social media election**'? In the immediate aftermath of the election, Piers Morgan asserted that 'Twitter loses another election'. While

Morgan is broadly right, the reality is more complex. Twitter's well-known liberal bias appears to reinforce views held by those in the metropolitan/media 'bubble', but the impact of private group chats on other social media platforms — there is evidence of group chats containing many thousands of 'persuadable' people within marginal constituencies — is considered to be rather more significant in shaping electoral outcomes.

Did the 2019 vote confirm first past the post's traditional strengths?

For many, MPs included, the first-past-the-post system is seen as the most appropriate electoral system to support the UK's democracy, its style of government and its parliamentary arrangements. It has been used to decide the outcome of UK elections for several centuries, withstanding the test of time despite its apparent flaws. The outcome of the 2019 general election led many to conclude that after almost a decade of inconclusive results, FPTP had returned to what it does best — delivering strong, single-party governments that hold clear mandates.

Strength 1: first past the post is easy to understand and results are declared quickly

- First past the post is one of the simplest electoral systems in operation with no complex formulas or quotas required to calculate winners. The candidates who receive the most votes in each constituency, needing just one more vote than their nearest rivals, are returned to Parliament. On Friday 13 December 2019, considerably less than 24 hours after the polls had closed, all of the UK's constituencies had declared their results (see Table 9.2).
- Unlike in 2010, when coalition talks between the Conservatives and Liberal Democrats lasted for 5 days, by midday on Friday 13 December — just 14 hours after polls had closed — Boris Johnson had visited the queen to receive a formal invitation to form a government.

Strength 2: first past the post leads to effective relationships between MPs and their constituencies, with clear accountability

- FPTP's use of single-member constituencies provides two main strengths. First, unlike the multi-member constituencies that are required by systems delivering broadly proportional results, there is complete clarity on who each constituency MP is, what each one stands for, and how each one votes and performs. Second, for MPs deemed to be inadequate or to defy the will of the majority of constituents, it is relatively easy to hold them to account and vote them out of office.
- In 2019 there were a number of high profile casualties, undone by the ease with which constituency MPs can be defeated by determined opposition under first past the post. Ex-Conservative minister and Brexit-backer Zac Goldsmith lost his Richmond Park seat, defeated by Remain-supporting Liberal Democrat Sarah Olney. Liberal Democrat leader Jo Swinson was replaced by the SNP's candidate, with Swinson accused of spending too much time on the national campaign trail and too little in her own constituency.

Table 9.2 Results of the 2019 general election

Party	Seats	Gains	Losses	Net	Vote share (%)	Change (%)	Total votes
Conservative	365	75	9	+66	43.6	+1.2	13,966,565
Labour	202	13	55	−42	32.2	−7.8	10,295,607
Scottish National Party	48	14	1	+13	3.9	+0.8	1,242,372
Liberal Democrat	11	3	13	−10	11.6	+4.2	3,696,423
Democratic Unionist Party	8	0	2	−2	0.8	−0.1	244,128
Sinn Féin	7	1	1	+0	0.6	−0.2	181,853
Plaid Cymru	4	0	0	+0	0.5	+0	153,265
Social Democratic and Labour Party	2	2	0	+2	0.4	+0.1	118,737
Green	1	0	0	+0	2.7	+1.1	865,697
Alliance	1	1	0	+1	0.4	+0.2	134,115
Brexit	0	0	0	+0	2	+2	642,303
Independent	0	0	23	−23	0.6	+0.2	196,843
Change	0	0	5	−5	0	+0	10,006
Other	0	0	0	+0	0.8	−1.6	264,000

Box 9.2 What are the strengths of single member constituencies?

Multi-member constituencies — the larger the better — provide balanced representation, not just in terms of the accurate translation of votes to seats but also according to other factors such as gender, ethnicity and age. Single-member constituencies have other strengths that are more widely appreciated by the UK electorate. Single-member constituencies provide close links between elected representatives and the geographic locations and constituents that they represent. Not only does this mean that the UK is well represented in a geographical sense, but that every vote is of identical value — one vote for one constituency candidate for each voter.

Strength 3: first past the post delivers decisive results and stable governments

- Arguably the most significant strength of FPTP is that it delivers decisive single party majority governments. As a result, the winning party is able to set about immediately fulfilling its manifesto commitments and can be held singularly accountable for its success or failure at the following election.
- The formation of a Conservative/Liberal Democrat coalition in 2010 led to uncertainty over which party was responsible for which policy failure. Theresa

May's minority government formed in 2017 was able to blame its ineffective execution of Brexit on its lack of a parliamentary majority.

- In 2019 however, within hours of the polls closing, Boris Johnson could legitimately claim that he led a single party 'people's government' able to unite to 'find closure' and 'let the healing begin'. The Conservative government's legitimacy was based on its haul of 365 seats (56% of the total) rather than its minority of national support (see Table 9.3).

Table 9.3 Decisive results delivered by first past the post: 9 single party government majorities in 11 elections in 40 years

Year	Winning party	Majority
1979	Conservative	43
1983	Conservative	144
1987	Conservative	102
1992	Conservative	29
1997	Labour	179
2001	Labour	167
2005	Labour	66
2010	Conservative	−36
2015	Conservative	12
2017	Conservative	−16
2019	Conservative	80

Strength 4: first past the post supports a two-party system at the expense of independents and 'extremists'

- The Liberal Democrats routinely suffer at the hands of FPTP. A directly proportional votes-to-seats translation in 2019 would have rewarded their 11.6% vote share with 75 seats. Similarly, FPTP does not reward minor parties and independent candidates that are unable to find sufficiently concentrated support to win individual seats.
- In 2019 the Brexit Party polled over 640,000 votes nationally: 2% of the total vote would have led to 13 seats in a directly proportional system. Supporters of FPTP claim that this allows the UK to marginalise groups that harvest discontented support for a short period of time, but that are unable to secure the legitimacy of a parliamentary seat.
- Additionally in 2019, the two main parties received 568 of the 650 seats — 87% of all seats in the House of Commons from a 76% share of the vote. The system does not just create a strong government but ensures that the second largest party is able to form a credible opposition. The Labour Party polled just over 32% of the vote and received 31% (202) of the seats.

2019 and the Liberal Democrats

The Liberal Democrats had one of their worst election campaigns on record. It was made all the more disappointing for them by the pre-election expectations of significant gains based on a campaign pledge of reversing the UK's impending departure from the EU without a public vote.

The Liberal Democrats may have polled 3.7 million votes (up over 4% on 2017) but lost 13 of the seats they held prior to the election and gained just 3, emerging from the polls with 11 MPs. Leader Jo Swinson lost her seat in Dunbartonshire East by just 149 votes and stepped down as Liberal Democrat leader.

Box 9.4 **2019 and independent candidates**

Another strength, or weakness, of FPTP depending on perspective, is the way that it concentrates party support to prevent independent and fringe-party candidates from gaining representation, thereby preserving the two-party cohesion of the parliamentary system.

2019 was little different with some very high profile candidates attempting to buck trends by securing seats on independent or fringe-party tickets. Examples include:

- Former Conservative ministers David Gauke, Dominic Grieve and Anne Milton, standing as independent candidates after they had the whip removed for voting in Parliament to block a no-deal Brexit, lost their seats.
- The four candidates who stood for the Independent Group for Change (former Conservative MP Anna Soubry, and former Labour MPs Gavin Shuker, Chris Leslie and Mike Gapes) all lost their seats to candidates in their former parties.

Is it time to replace first past the post?

The main arguments for replacing FPTP lie in the fact that it is both unfair and unrepresentative in the way that it translates votes to seats. The 2019 election was no different in this regard, with the usual problems of distorted voting values, wasted votes and the preservation of safe seats.

Weakness 1: first past the post is fundamentally undemocratic

If the purpose of an election is to create a representative assembly based upon the wishes of the electorate, then the outcome of the 2019 election did not deliver on this. First past the post is a constituency-based system, requiring winning candidates to secure just one more vote (a simple majority) than their nearest rival. Consequently many candidates in 2019 won their seats with significantly less than 50% of the vote, and 29 winning margins were under 1,000 votes.

> ### Box 9.5 | 2019: narrow constituency victories
>
> - Bury North's new Conservative MP James Daly has the UK's narrowest majority of just 105 after winning the seat from Labour incumbent James Frith. James Daly polled 21,660 votes to James Frith's 21,555.
> - The Liberal Democrats held the Scottish seat of Caithness, Sutherland and Easter Ross with 37.2% of the constituency vote and a majority of just 204. 19,752 votes went to the four other candidates but count for nothing.

Narrow wins and low shares of the vote for winning candidates build up to a national picture that allows a 'winning' party, with just 43.6%, to secure a sizeable majority of seats in the House of Commons.

Weakness 2: first past the post distorts voting values

The large number of wasted votes — those won by candidates and parties that do not contribute to the electing of a representative — distort voting values. FPTP is a 'winner-takes-all' system meaning that both the size of the winner's majority and all the votes for losing candidates can lead to serious electoral anomalies and accusations that the system is undemocratic. Examples include:

- On a constituency level, some margins of victory are far in excess of the amount required. In Liverpool Walton, Labour MP Dan Carden held the seat with 84.7% in 2019, more than 30,000 votes ahead of his nearest rival.
- On a national basis, the pile-up of wasted votes — either votes for losing candidates or over-large constituency majorities — can distort voting values. Liberal Democrats received a seat for every 336,038 votes they secured, whereas the Conservatives received a seat for every 38,264 votes (see Table 9.4)

Table 9.4 How many votes did it take to elect an MP in 2019?

Party*	Votes	Seats	Voters per seat
Conservative	13,966,565	365	38,264
Labour	10,295,607	202	50,968
Liberal Democrat	3,696,423	11	336,038
Scottish Nationalist	1,242,372	48	25,882
Green	865,697	1	865,697
Brexit	642,303	0	n/a

*Parties polling more than 250,000 votes

Weakness 3: first past the post does not create a representative assembly

Quickly following most general election analysis is what the results *might* have been if a form of proportional representation had been used. Needless to say, any such analysis is highly questionable as voters cast their votes knowing how the system operates: if a different system were in use, offering different outcomes, then many voters would cast their votes in different ways.

On the day following the 2019 result, the Electoral Reform Society revealed that if the UK had used the voting system adopted for European Parliament elections

Boris Johnson would have been denied a parliamentary majority. The Electoral Reform Society asserted that under the regional list proportional representation system:

- The Conservatives would have won 77 fewer seats.
- Labour would have won 14 more.
- The Greens Party would have added another 11 MPs to its 2019 total of just 1.
- The Liberal Democrats would have been the biggest gainers, taking 59 more seats to win at least 70 (see Table 9.5).

Following the 2019 vote, Darren Hughes, chief executive of the Electoral Reform Society explained: 'Westminster's voting system is warping our politics beyond recognition and we're all paying the price. Under proportional voting systems, seats would more closely match votes, and we could end the scourge of millions feeling unrepresented and ignored.'

Table 9.5 What the result of the 2019 general election would have looked like if proportional representation had been used

Party	First past the post	Regional list proportional representation	Seat change
Conservative	365	288	↓ 77
Labour	202	216	↑ 14
SNP	48	28	↓ 20
Liberal Democrat	11	70	↑ 59
DUP	8	6	↓ 2
Sinn Féin	7	4	↓ 3
Plaid Cymru	4	4	0
SDLP	2	3	↑ 1
Alliance	1	3	↑ 2
Others	1	4	↑ 3
Green Party	1	12	↑ 11
Brexit Party	0	10	↑ 10
UUP	0	2	↑ 2

Source: Electoral Reform Society, December 2019

Weakness 4: first past the post results in safe seats and uncompetitive elections

One of the major criticisms of FPTP is that the system entrenches safe seats. In a safe seat, the same party candidate is routinely returned with an almost insurmountable majority. Voters can therefore feel disinclined to turn out to vote.

The Electoral Reform Society asserts that the seat of Shropshire North has been in the hands of the Conservatives for almost two centuries. In 2019, Shropshire North duly remained in the hands of Conservative MP Owen Patterson, with a turnout of 62.7%, 5% below the national turnout figure. Shropshire North is one of almost 250 seats that have not changed hands for more than 70 years. Thirty of those pre-date 1900.

Summary

The extent to which the relative bluntness of the first-past-the-post electoral system still serves the UK effectively remains a subject of significant debate. However, the level of engagement and willingness for people to vote in local contests where 'every vote counts' (the turnout in Dunbartonshire East that saw Liberal Democrat leader Jo Swinson lose her seat was over 80%), demonstrates the robustness of a system that has survived for centuries.

Analysis and evaluation from the 2019 general election needs to be placed alongside other debates such as:

- What is the primary purpose of elections — to deliver as accurate an assembly as possible or to provide the country with an effective government?
- Is the marginalisation of minor party candidates, ensuring that parties like the Greens never gain a true foothold of legitimate parliamentary representation, possible to support?
- Do other voting systems bring greater strengths or just a different set of advantages and disadvantages?

What next?

Read:

- Jonathan Birth's article, 'Five reasons to vote in a safe seat', on the London School of Economics blog (**https://blogs.lse.ac.uk**)
- BBC media editor Amol Rajan's article 'General election 2019: Five lessons from the 'social media' election' (**www.bbc.co.uk**)

Chapter 10

What factors determined the outcome of the 2019 general election and why?

Exam success

A thorough understanding of the factors that influence electoral outcomes and that shape voting behaviour is a central feature of the examination specifications. Students need to be able to analyse the traditional significance of social class and its decline as a major shaper of voting behaviour, and the extent to which other factors and theories provide more effective explanations. Evaluating the importance of factors such as age, gender, ethnicity, region and rational choice or issue-based voting theories are required too. The best answers will be able to link factors and theories with examples from specific elections, providing high level analysis as to how and why attitudes towards policy issues, election campaigns and leaders are increasingly shaping electoral outcomes.

Edexcel	UK Politics 4.1 and 4.2	Case studies of general elections and the factors that explain their outcomes including analysis of voting behaviour and the influence of the media
AQA	3.1.2.2	Studies of general elections including factors that influence their outcomes such as policies, campaigns, leadership and the electoral system itself

Context

Members of the voting public are frequently encouraged to view every voting opportunity as a 'once in a generation' event. In this regard, the 2019 general election was just like the 2017 election, the 2016 referendum on EU membership, and the 2014 Scottish independence referendum: all of them singular opportunity for voters to finally 'get their voices heard'.

However, understanding the complex motivation of voters is challenging, and has been a preoccupation of academics and researchers for as long as voting has existed. Indeed psephology, the study of voting behaviour, takes its name from the Greek word *psephos*, a pebble, dropped by the ancient Greeks into urns to cast their votes. Nowadays, just as in classical times, the behaviour of voters is influenced by a vast array of different and sometimes contradictory factors.

Added to that are the significant structural changes over the past 50 years in the prevailing influences upon voting behaviour. The 1940s to 1970s were characterised by the period of postwar consensus (broad agreement on a balance between nationalised industries, government regulation and generous welfare provision) and a healthy relationship between class and party. Since then, a period of partisan dealignment has occurred that has seen other factors and motivators supplant class as the most important indicator of voting behaviour. These include long-term (primacy) factors such as region, race, gender and age and short-term (recency) factors that place an increasing importance on party leaders, and on prevailing attitudes towards key issues such as welfare, education and environmental policies.

Overall, there is little doubt that voters are more 'rational' and less sentimental or conventional in the way that they cast their votes, and 2019 saw victory for the party that was able to engage with this ever-evolving trend far more effectively than the others.

Box 10.1 Key definitions

Partisan dealignment: the increasing tendency of voters to support particular parties not because of their socioeconomic status, but according to a far wider range of subjective and objective factors. In other words, class has become a far weaker indicator of which way a person will vote.

Rational choice models of voting behaviour: these emphasise that people are far less committed to a particular party or ideology than they used to be. They are far more likely to establish which party's ideas are aligned to theirs and which leaders appear to offer solutions to issues that they feel particularly strongly about.

What voting patterns lay behind the Conservative Party's win?

Boris Johnson's 2019 general election victory made him the most powerful leader since Tony Blair. The Conservative Party's 80-seat majority is the largest governing lead since New Labour's victory in 2001, and the strongest Conservative government majority since the late 1980s. Almost 14 million people voted in favour of the Conservatives in 2019, well over 3.5 million more than voted for the Labour Party. However, behind the figures lie trends that are far from uniform across the country and require deeper analysis:

1 The Brexit bonus

In the 2019 general election the Conservative Party enjoyed a relatively modest increase in its percentage of the national vote (up just 1.2% from 2017). Within this though, there were dramatically different swings across constituencies. While comparisons can be drawn with previous landslide victories, it is worth keeping in mind that the Tories secured a net gain of just 47 seats in 2019, gaining 57 seats from 2017 but losing 10. When Tony Blair won New Labour's landslide in 1997, his party's vote share went up by 8.8% and it gained 145 seats.

So, different factors are at work in different locations, and in 2019, this was in large part down to the relative support for Leave and Remain in each constituency. Polling indicates that:

- In seats where more than 60% of voters backed Leave in the 2016 EU referendum, the Conservative Party saw an average rise in support of 6%.
- In seats where 60% voted Remain, the Conservative Party's vote fell by three points.

Box 10.2 **Leave v Remain — splits that benefited the Conservative Party**

Those who voted Leave in the 2016 referendum voted overwhelmingly for the Conservatives (73% in the Ashcroft election day poll). Meanwhile there was a split among Remain voters — 20% Conservative, 47% Labour and 21% Lib Dem — and a similar split, too, among those who did not vote in the referendum.

Steven Fisher, *Prospect Magazine*, December 2019

Magnifying the Conservative Party's 'Brexit bonus' was the fact that the Labour Party's particularly unpopular approach to Brexit saw the party's vote decline by an average of 10.4% in strong Leave constituencies (compared to 7.9% overall).

2 Breaching the 'red wall'

There is little doubt that strong support in solidly Leave-supporting areas formed the backbone of the Conservative Party's election victory. For many Leave supporters, evasion and delay in Westminster had increased their sense of dissatisfaction and disillusionment. In the end, MPs who had frustrated the process, who had quarrelled and resigned from their parties in dispute, who had formed alliances to overturn the referendum result, where almost all swept away. In particular, despite Tory gains at large, David Gauke, Dominic Grieve and Anne Milton — former Conservative ministers who stood as independents after having had the whip removed for blocking a no-deal Brexit — all lost their seats.

In addition to these individual MPs, and in one of the most startling developments of the election, Leave-supporting seats in the Midlands and North, many of which had never before voted Conservative, 'turned blue'. Wrexham, Workington, Blyth Valley, across the West Midlands, Yorkshire, Lancashire and into the Northeast were seats that had evaded even Margaret Thatcher's 1980s landslides but that were won by the Conservative Party in 2019.

Box 10.3 **Breaching the 'Red Wall'**

- Labour veteran Dennis Skinner had held the Bolsover seat for 49 years. Skinner, at 87-years old, was set to become the Father of the House — the longest serving MP following Ken Clarke's retirement — but saw his vote share decline by 16% and he lost the seat to the Conservative Party.
- Another solidly Labour seat was Tony Blair's former constituency of Sedgefield. Held with a majority of more than 25,000 in 1997, in 2019 the Conservatives won the seat with more than 4,500 votes.
- Elsewhere, Rother Valley had been a Labour seat since 1918 but the Conservatives overturned a 3,882 majority to win it by 6,318 votes.
- Bassetlaw in Nottinghamshire was won by the Conservatives from Labour in the biggest swing of the night as the Labour Party vote fell by over 24%.

---

3 One-nation conservatism

There was plainly more to the Conservative Party victory than Brexit. 2019 also demonstrated that the link between the Labour Party and its traditional working-class base had changed markedly.

In the 2019 election, Labour support fell further than average in constituencies with most voters in working-class jobs — by an average of 11%. While there is a strong link between working-class voters and Leave voters, there was also widespread disdain in former Labour heartlands for the direction that the Labour Party had moved in.

Box 10.4	Perspectives on Labour's detachment from its working-class base

That Boris Johnson now commands all he surveys is entirely down to the collapse of the 'red wall' — former Labour strongholds that found themselves utterly detached from the neo-Marxist, spendaholic, Europhile, uber-woke, London-luvvie Labour Party under the leadership of a teetotal vegetarian fan of Hamas.

Robert Hardman, *Daily Mail*, 14 December 2019

The next leader needs to understand the communities that gave birth to the labour movement and realise that the whole country is not very like Labour London. As important as it is, too often, Labour addresses the metropolitan wing of its electoral coalition in terms of values — openness, tolerance, human rights — and the 'traditional' working-class wing simply in terms of a material offer, as if their constituencies did not have their own values of solidarity and community. That must change.

Len McCluskey, General Secretary of the Unite Union,
Huffington Post UK, 13 December 2019

In contrast, an evidently more appealing and optimistic message was delivered by Boris Johnson. Not simply a resolution to 'get Brexit done', but — among other campaign pledges — a determined bid to redress the balance between London and the North. For some, it was 'classic One-Nation conservatism', an appeal to the entire country, cutting across class divides with paternalistic policies and an expectation that the wealthy should assist the less well off.

Box 10.5	Boris Johnson's appeal to new Conservative voters

In this moment of national resolution I want to speak directly to those who made it possible, and to those who voted for us for the first time and those whose pencils may have wavered over the ballot and who heard the voices of their parents and grandparents whispering anxiously in their ears.

I say: thank you for the trust you have placed in us and in me.

We will work around the clock to repay your trust and to deliver on your priorities with a Parliament that works for you.

Boris Johnson, 13 December 2019

Confirming the support that the Conservatives won from working class voters is a Lord Ashcroft poll of 13,000 people on election day who had already cast their vote. Three striking features of the poll include:

1 Labour won more than half the vote among those turning out aged 18–24 (57%) and 25–34 (55%). The Conservatives were ahead among those aged 45–54 (43%), 55–64 (49%) and 65+ (62%).

2 Men voted with the Conservatives by a 19-point margin of Labour (48% to 29%), while women did so by just six points (42% to 36%).

3 The Conservatives were the most supported among all socioeconomic groups by margins of between 6 points (DEs – working class and non-working voters) and 20 points (C2s – skilled working class voters).

4 The Conservative campaign

With an increasingly volatile electorate it is little surprise that voters make their minds up ever later in the campaign. According to the Lord Ashcroft exit poll in 2019, more than half of voters said that they made up their minds within the last month. A quarter said they did so within the last few days.

Consequently, the campaign – and its messaging – takes on an even greater importance. A number of features of the Conservative Party campaign in 2019 have been cited as being significant in shaping voting behaviour and, ultimately, the outcome of the election:

- The three-word slogan 'Get Brexit done' was the idea of key strategist Dominic Cummings. It resonated in the same way the famous EU referendum three-word-phrase 'Take back control' did.
- Other often repeated campaign slogan's such as 'Unleash Britain's potential' made a far more positive impact than Labour's quickly forgotten 'It's time for real change'.
- Both Conservative and Labour manifesto spending proposals were robustly critiqued by the Institute for Fiscal Studies (IFS), but it may well have been criticism of the Labour Party's spending pledges that hit hardest among voters. The IFS effectively declared Labour's tax and spending plans to be undeliverable.
- Pragmatic approaches to silence perceived electoral liabilities such as Jacob Rees-Mogg were effective.
- The removal of Brexit Party candidates from Conservative seats meant that resources could focus on key marginals.
- Boris Johnson's refusal to be interviewed by Andrew Neil was less harmful than Jeremy Corbyn's appearance, during which he refused to apologise for the Party's handling of anti-Semitism.
- The media assumed that media-based events would have a greater impact on the voting public than they did. In the end, the frenzy over the *Daily Mirror*'s photograph of a boy on a hospital floor, and the outrage at Boris Johnson's failure to appear on a Channel 4 debate about climate change, seemed to have little actual impact on voters.

Why did the Labour Party lose the 2019 general election?

The result of the 2019 general election stands out as much for the Conservative victory as for the disastrous performance of the Labour Party. To have lost four successive general elections within 9 years is a significant feat in itself, but to do so against a backdrop of Conservative-led government malfunction and public service austerity, and with odds seemingly stacked heavily in favour of any credible opposition, is widely considered to be exceptional.

Box 10.6 How bad was the 2019 general election defeat for the Labour Party?

In 2019 the party won fewer seats that it did in the 1983 general election, a previous low point. Then, despite the media dubbing its manifesto the 'longest suicide note in history' Labour won 209 seats, 7 more than it did in 2019. The last time the party won fewer than 200 seats was in 1935.

The days following the general election were characterised by disappointment and bitter recrimination within the Labour Party. Reasons for its catastrophic defeat include the following:

1 Jeremy Corbyn's personal unpopularity

'Not Brexit but Corbyn' asserted many senior Labour figures, including Edinburgh South MP Ian Murray, in the hours after polls closed (Box 10.7). While the Labour leadership was quick to lay the blame of its defeat on Brexit (Box 10.8), a poll by Opinium asking voters why they had not backed Labour in the general election saw 'leadership' coming out on top at 43%, with 'Brexit' a distant second at 17% and economic policies at 12% (Figure 10.1).

Box 10.7 Not Brexit but Corbyn

Every door I knocked on, and my team and I spoke to 11,000 people, mentioned Corbyn. Not Brexit but Corbyn. I've been saying this for years. The outcome is that we've let the country down and we must change course and fast.

Ian Murray, Edinburgh South MP, 13 December 2019

Box 10.8 Party leaders blame Brexit for Labour's defeat

I have pride in our manifesto that we put forward, and all the policies we put forward, which actually had huge public support. But this election was taken over ultimately by Brexit and we as a party represent people who voted both Remain and Leave.

Labour leader Jeremy Corbyn to the BBC, 13 December 2019

We just couldn't get through the Brexit argument basically. I think on the policy issues we won the argument, but we literally couldn't break through Brexit.

Labour Shadow Chancellor John McDonnell to Sky News, 12 December 2019

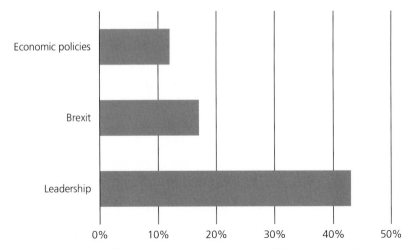

Figure 10.1 The main reasons why voters did not vote for the Labour Party in the 2019 general election

Opinium Exit Poll question to 5,000 voters, 12 December 2019

A Lord Ashcroft exit poll revealed that 49% of all voters said Boris Johnson would make the best prime minister, with 31% naming Jeremy Corbyn. Praise for Jeremy Corbyn's 'decency' among many, often younger, Labour party supporters was at odds with his negative perception at large. According to an Ipsos Mori poll, the Labour leader's satisfaction ratings going into the election campaign were lower than that of any opposition leader since the 1970s. Ultimately, Corbyn found it impossible to shake off his association with terrorist causes such as the Irish republican movement, cited by many voters, according to Labour Party canvassers, during the campaign.

2 Anti-Semitism

Sustained allegations of anti-Semitism had been levelled at the Labour Party for over 4 years. In the 8 months between April 2018 and January 2019, the party received almost 700 complaints related to anti-Semitism. Despite setting up an independent enquiry into the prevalence of anti-Semitism within the party in 2016, Jeremy Corbyn failed to convince large sections of the public that he was serious about dealing with the matter.

The Labour leader's refusal to apologise for his handling of the problem during an election interview with Andrew Neil in December 2019 baffled and angered many voters. Shadow Chancellor John McDonnell, 4 days before the general election, voiced his concerns about the public reaction to anti-Semitism within the party: 'I worry this has had an effect.'

Box 10.9   Resignations of MPs and peers over anti-Semitism

In 2019, resignations over anti-Semitism reached peak proportions:

- February 2019: seven MPs resigned from the Labour Party to form The Independent Group for Change citing their discontent with Labour's political direction, approach to Brexit and to allegations of anti-Semitism within the party.
- July 2019: three members of the House of Lords, David Triesman, Leslie Arnold Turnberg and Ara Darzi, resigned the Labour whip, citing dissatisfaction with the party's handling of anti-Semitism, Brexit and defence policy.
- October 2019: Louise Ellman MP resigned from the party, citing her worries about anti-Semitism in the party.

3 Brexit

In blaming Brexit for the defeat, the Labour leadership failed to fully consider the impact of their own approach to the issue. Labour adopted a policy of seeking to renegotiate a Brexit deal with the EU within 3 months and to put that deal, along with a choice to remain, to a public vote within 6 months. Many Leave-supporting voters felt let down by an approach that, along with further delay, would almost certainly have seen a 'soft Brexit v Remain' referendum. For many senior Labour Party figures, however much they might have wanted to overturn the 2016 referendum result, the policy was not just ambiguous but anti-democratic (Box 10.10).

Box 10.10   How Labour's Brexit policy become its undoing

What we are seeing in the Labour heartlands is people very aggrieved at the fact the party basically has taken a stance on Brexit the way they have. Ignoring the wishes of 17.4 million voters was not a good recipe: ignore democracy and to be quite honest the consequences will come back and bite you up the backside.

Labour Party Chairman Ian Lavery to the BBC, 13 December 2019

4 Manifesto commitments and campaign strategy

Miscalculation and misassumptions were hallmarks of the Labour Party's wider vision and electoral strategy. The surge in support in the final weeks of the 2017 general election campaign proved to be the party's undoing, convincing party leaders that despite all indicators to the contrary, radical policies and huge spending commitments would deliver a similar late wave.

Ultimately, Labour's massive spending commitments and renationalisation projects were unconvincing. Policy giveaways such as 'free broadband', landed on suspicious voters without any context. And realisation came too late that the socially conservative 'red wall' of formerly solidly Labour seats in the Midlands and North had been taken for granted in favour of policies that played better to more liberally minded, urban voters. For many senior Labour figures such as David Blunkett, the direction that the Labour Party took, with its bitter internal divisions between those loyal to the Corbyn-supporting Momentum movement and those not, was the root cause of Labour's disastrous defeat.

Box 10.11 Blame for the Labour Party's failure

Andrew Neil lambasts Laura Parker, Momentum's national coordinator:

> What didn't work was Jeremy Corbyn! You were told by Labour Party people that Jeremy Corbyn was unelectable but the Momentum cult wouldn't listen. You've been thrashed! You took control of the Labour Party and the Labour Party has been thrashed. It's been a disastrous experiment for you.
>
> Source: BBC interview, 13 December 2019

Former Labour Home Secretary Alan Johnson blames Momentum founder Jon Lansman for his part in Labour's defeat:

> I don't live in London, I live in Yorkshire, in a working-class community and I've known Jon Lansman for many years. Jon's been around from the Bennite days. The working classes have always been a big disappointment to Jon and his cult. Corbyn was a disaster on the doorstep. Everyone knew he couldn't lead the working class out of a paper bag.
>
> Source: ITV interview, 13 December 2019

Summary

Among other things, this chapter provides analysis of factors that may have influenced the outcome of the general election — four factors for the Conservatives and four for Labour. Each factor is open to dispute and debate, but may go some way towards explaining the substantial 11.2% polling difference between the two main parties. Needless to say, there were many other factors at play — some of them based purely on voting mechanics. While assuming uniform switches of allegiance based on Leave-Remain is unwise:

- The Brexit Party withdrew from contesting existing Conservative seats, but its 640,000+ votes were highly concentrated in a relatively small number of pro-Leave seats. In particular, among the first seats to declare, such as those of Labour-held Houghton and Sunderland South and Washington and Sunderland West, votes for the Brexit Party were far greater than the difference between the Conservatives and the winning Labour Party candidate.
- Even more emphatic were the 'wasted' votes for many Liberal Democrat candidates, ones that failed to elect a Liberal Democrat MP but that played a part in determining a constituency outcome. In many Remain-supporting regions, votes for the Liberal Democrats were far greater than the difference between those gained by the Labour Party and the winning Conservative Party candidate.

The role played by the media — whether 'traditional' mainstream media, such as the BBC, ITV, Sky News, and print journalism, or 'new' media and the effective manipulation of social media platforms — is a significant area that requires further attention too. The experiences of the party leaders were far from uniform and the extent to which this played a part in the election outcome, as well as the impact of disinformation and determined vilification of high-profile figures, requires evaluation. For further analysis of the role of the media read the following articles:

- 'What we learned about the media this election' by the *Guardian*'s media editor, Jim Waterson, 15 December 2019, which analyses whether 2019 saw unprecedented levels of media criticism (**www.theguardian.com**)
- 'Online political advertising in the UK 2019 general election campaign' by Emma Goodman, 12 December 2019 (**https://blogs.lse.ac.uk**)
- 'General election 2019: How *The Sun*, *Daily Mail*, *Daily Mirror* and other papers went all out to sway voters' by Padraic Flanagan, 12 December 2019 (**https://inews.co.uk/news**)
- 'The media's influence on voting behaviour' by Rowena Hammal, *Politics Review,* Volume 29, Issue 2

The voting patterns exhibited in the 2019 general election are part of a wider debate on the changing shape of voting habits in the UK; the shifting influence of social class, partisanship, longer-term social factors such as gender and age, and shorter-term rational issues such as the importance of the leadership, the economy and — of course in 2019 — Brexit.

What next?

In understanding the factors behind the Conservative Party's win, see also:

- Lord Ashcroft's exit poll on the Conservative Home website (**www.conservativehome.com**) under 'How Britain voted and why. My 2019 post-vote poll'
- Stephen Fisher's explanation for the factors behind the Conservative win on Prospect's website (**www.prospectmagazine.co.uk**) under 'How did the Conservatives win?'
- Sir John Curtice's analysis on the BBC website (**www.bbc.co.uk**) under 'General Election 2019: What's behind the Conservative victory?'